**"From henceforth thou shalt take men alive."**

Luke 5:10

"Taking men alive" for Christ is still the chief responsibility and privilege of Christians. For if men are not "taken alive" for Christ, they will be taken alive for Satan.

As this Charles G. Trumbull classic profoundly illustrates, the best way to win men to Christ is to lead them to Him one by one. It was our Lord's own method; it was the method of His apostles; and it has been the method of the greatest soul-winners from His day until now. The beauty of this form of evangelism is that everyone can do it. While we all may not be great preachers or gifted Bible teachers, we all can be, and should be, enthusiastic witnesses to the One who has brought us out of death unto life. May the profound insights provided in *Taking Men Alive* inspire you to make individual soul-winning a way of life.

# TAKING MEN ALIVE

## CHARLES G. TRUMBULL

**Power Books**

Fleming H. Revell Company
Old Tappan, New Jersey

Scripture quotations used in this volume are taken from the King James Version of the Bible.

Library of Congress Cataloging-in-Publication Data

Trumbull, Charles G. (Charles Gallaudet), 1872-1941.
    Talking men alive: the principles and practice of winning men for
Jesus Christ/Charles G. Trumbull.
        p.  cm.
    Includes bibliographical references.
    ISBN 0-8007-5375-5
    1. Evangelistic work.   2. Witness bearing (Christianity)
I. Title.
BV3790.T692 1990
269'.2—dc20                                                90-41521
                                                                CIP

Published by the Fleming H. Revell Company
Old Tappan, New Jersey 07675
Printed in the United States of America

# Contents

# Foreword

T*AKING MEN ALIVE* is a remarkable book. Published in 1905 about the principles of personal evangelism used by a Civil War chaplain, you might think it hopelessly out-of-date. Instead I've found it to be a classic.

Three years ago a businessman asked me for help in personal witnessing. I looked over some of the superb books available today. While doing so, I reexamined my copy of *Taking Men Alive*, which had helped me so much years ago. After describing its contents to my businessman friend we decided to take a chapter a week, write out answers to the questions both at the beginning and end of each chapter, and discuss them.

While some of the language is different from today, we found the material amazingly helpful. So helpful that we began to tell other businessmen about it. But no copies could be found anywhere. Consequently, my friend duplicated fifty copies. Those gradually were put to use in one-to-one situations all over the country.

Finally, a businessman from Little Rock, Arkansas, said, "This is so helpful we need to see if Fleming Revell will republish it." Revell agreed to republish their edition, which was revised by the author in 1938. So here I am, writing an introduction to a classic on personal evangelism.

Today we talk about evangelism as a life-style. It is not just something one does on Tuesday nights; it is something to do all the time. Wherever, one must be on the alert for an opportunity to say a word about their experience of Jesus. This is a ministry for the home place, the workplace, and the social place. In short—every place.

To do that well, a person must know how to use limited time opportunities. He must learn to recognize those opportunities, how to use them, and when to stop. *Taking Men Alive* is an outstanding help in learning how to do that.

From Mr. Trumbull you will learn the need of a life-resolve, the right preparation, the right approach and the right follow-through. It will be something you can do in your daily life without adding another program to your schedule. You will also learn:

1. It is the greatest work you can do.
2. It is the hardest work you can do.
3. It is the most rewarding work you can do.

Don't just read this book through. Find a friend who also wants to take men alive. Agree to take a chapter a week. Write out the answers to the questions at the beginning and end of each chapter. Then meet together in person, or by phone, and discuss your answers. Pray together for opportunities to practice what you are learning and share your experiences at your next meeting. It will electrify you both.

When you have completed the book, each of you find another person with whom you can repeat the process and thereby multiply the laborers in the harvest.

Dr. Lorne C. Sanny

# Introduction

**M**EN still need to be won to Christ. "Taking men alive" for Christ is still the chief responsibility and privilege of Christians. For if men are not "taken alive" for Christ, they will be "taken alive" for Satan; the Greek verb meaning "to take alive" occurs only twice in the New Testament, in one case meaning capturing men unto eternal life, in the other, Satan's capture of men unto eternal death.

And the best way of winning men to Christ is to lead them to Him one by one. It was our Lord's own method; it was the method of His apostles; and it has been the method of the greatest soul-winners from His day until now. The beauty of this form of evangelism is that everyone can do it. Few can be great preachers, few are gifted Bible teachers; all can be, and should be, witnesses to the One who has brought them out of death into life.

It was undoubtedly the usual practice among the early Christians to tell others with whom they had daily contact in the pagan or heathen world around them of the death and resurrection of Jesus Christ, the Son of God and Savior of sinners, and to tell what He had done for them and what He meant to them in their personal life and experience. There is as great a need of this today as in the first century—even greater.

\* \* \*

On the eighth of December 1903, a great printing press was awaiting a message that should carry, to the hundred thousand readers of the paper which it was to print, the news of the death of its editor. The one who, in that moment of grief and uncertainty, must write the message, tried to view the seventy-three years of life that had just closed, the half-century of manhood that had ministered unceasingly. The life was rich in varied and extended forms of service: as home missionary in Sunday school work, as army chaplain, as interpreter of the Bible, as traveler and explorer, as preacher and speaker and editor, and as writer of more than thirty volumes in the field of character building and spiritual truth.

Yet in that hour when death seems to reveal the real man and his central power and purpose, the one form of ministry that stood out in clearest light to those who knew this man best was the ministry of which the world at large, though it knew him well, knew least. It was his self-sacrificing service for the individual; his instant and invariable putting of the claims of one above the claims of many; his sinking and spending all that he had and all that he was in order to serve the one-at-a-time for whom he lived.

And so the message that told of the earthly ending of his life was the message that the whole life had spoken; and the summons was sounded, to all who loved him, to "make his past a success" by carrying on his greatest work, the winning of individuals to Christ. And it is significant that one of the least pretentious of the thirty volumes that Henry Clay Trumbull wrote is proving to be the most influential of them all in far-reaching blessing—the little book that tells the simple narrative of his "Individual Work for Individuals."

A few months after the death of Dr. Trumbull, the writer was asked to conduct a class at the annual convention of the

Brotherhood of Andrew and Philip, in the study of "Individual Work for Individuals," on the basis of the experiences set down by his father in the volume on that subject.

The idea of using that book as a textbook for class study was a new one, for it had not been written with just that end in view. But the wealth of material for study that it contained was unquestionable. So the experiment was tried; and every one who had a part in it was, apparently, surprised not only at the adaptability of the material to a classification by principles, but also at the definiteness and simplicity of the several principles which were clearly seen to be at the foundation of the success of the work that Dr. Trumbull did. Laymen and ministers in that summer study-class who had already been familiar with the contents of the little volume, and yet who had never sought to ascertain the principles of work which it does not specifically mention, but which it abundantly reveals, expressed themselves as impressed with the importance and the gain of this new view of the work.

In the years that have passed since then, the writer has been privileged to test the studies of that summer on more than a score of occasions, with both large and small audiences, in ten different states and provinces of North America. Sometimes but a single session has been devoted to the subject; again, a small group of students has met for three or four consecutive class sessions, ready for thorough investigation. In Brotherhood, Sunday school, and Christian Endeavor conventions, church prayer meetings, a men's guild, a university students' Christian association, church congregations, and theological seminaries in Pennsylvania, New Jersey, Kentucky, and Tennessee, the principles have been presented, worked out, challenged, discussed, and often unexpectedly illuminated by those who have brought their own fruitful experiences to bear. The material that has gone into the following pages is the result of these years of study and conference.

H. Clay Trumbull's *Individual Work for Individuals* is chiefly a record of actual experiences, grouped by chronological periods in the life of its writer, and intended primarily to show what God is willing to do for one who seeks to improve daily opportunities of extending His invitation. It was not the purpose of that book to make a special study of the principles underlying the art of witnessing. It is easy to miss those principles unless one specifically looks for them, and, missing them, to fail in the effectiveness that one might have and ought to have. The ascertaining, formulating, and illustrating of such principles is the distinctive purpose of this book.

# The Work We Are Facing

## Questions to Ask Yourself Before You Read the Chapter

1. What is individual soul-winning? Formulate your own careful definition.
2. For whom is it a duty? Why?
3. From your own observation, what percentage of church members should you say engage in it?
4. As between minister and layman, who has the better opportunity to carry on this work?
5. Is the greatest proficiency in the work acquired, or a gift?
6. What form of Christian service would you consider greater than this?
7. To what facts and factors do you attribute the peculiar effectiveness of individual work?

# 1
# The Work We Are Facing

IF Jesus of Nazareth had not been a Master Fisherman, the work of extending His Kingdom among men would have ended with His death. If we do not learn and practice His art of fishing, or "taking men alive," we shall be failures in the chief work of His Kingdom on earth.

And the fishing unto eternal life must be done individually. Consider these three truths:

*The work of individual soul-winning is the greatest work that God permits men to do.*

*It was Christ's own preferred method of work, as it is His preferred method for us today. For it is always the most effective way of working.*

*It is the hardest work in the world to do, and it always will be the hardest.*

If we are not prepared to accept these statements as true, we shall have opportunity to investigate and test them as we go on with our studies. But, let us remember, every man in the world is going to be "taken alive"—by someone. The Greek *zogreo*, meaning "to take alive," occurs only twice in the entire New

Testament: in Luke 5:10 and 2 Timothy 2:26. In the one case, Jesus promises to enable His disciple to take men alive for the Kingdom. In the other case, Paul speaks of those who have been taken alive by the devil. It is the same word in both cases, but with what a different outcome! By one or the other fisher of men every soul will eventually be taken—taken alive unto death, or taken alive unto eternal life.

The basis of these studies will be the record of the experiences that one man had during fifty years of work as an individual soul-winner.[1] He seemed to have peculiar power and to be blessed with exceptional success in the work. This man was a layman throughout his life, and therefore he had no professional equipment such as the ordinary Christian worker lacks. He had a degree of D.D., to be sure, but that was purely honorary. He never was inside a theological seminary in his life, except as a visitor. He never even went to college. He had a rudimentary school education, and not much of that after four-teen years of age. He worked always and only as a man among men, never from any vantage point of professional or pulpit position. Even when performing the duties of an ordained army chaplain, he worked as a layman rather than as a chaplain.

He learned, amid the hard knocks of political and business life, and later as a Sunday school missionary and an army chaplain, that men are to be won in any field, whether that of merchandise, life insurance, or soul salvation, only in accor-dance with certain definite principles of man-winning. He *had* to learn what those principles were, or fail throughout. And he applied them to this chief business of life, as well as to its side issues.

## Individual Work the Greatest Work

That individual soul-winning is the greatest work that God calls men to do is simply part of the paradox-principle that runs through the entire Bible. A paradox is a seeming contradiction. We begin to meet it as soon as we begin to study the Bible. For there is a paradox at the very heart of things. The Way of Life is the great paradox of the universe. Here it is: "Whosoever will save his life shall lose it: but whosoever will lose his life for my sake, the same shall save it " (Luke 9:24). The Man who was to win the world must do so by being rejected of the world. He who saves from death by conquering death does so by Himself yielding to death. ". . . he that is least among you all, the same shall be great" (Luke 9:48). It is the sacrifice of the greater for the lesser, the worthy for the unworthy, the strong for the weak; not the loveless theory of the survival of the fittest, but instead the sacrifice of the fittest that the feeblest may survive. So it goes. The place of the paradox, or the seeming inversion of the natural order, is so firmly rooted in all our Christian life and studies that it needs no argument or proof.

That one is more than many is simply in line with this eternal principle. You cannot reach a thousand unless you can reach one. The greatest preaching in the world is the preaching to an individual. The world is never going to be brought to Christ wholesale, but one by one. Men are not born collectively; they do not die collectively; they do not accept or reject Christ collectively.

But it is not yet recognized as generally as it should be that the leading of a single soul to Christ is rarely accomplished by a general or a pulpit appeal.

> It is not enough for us to cry out a message to those who may hear, or who may not; to those who may understand it, or who may not. We have a hearer to win as well as a hearer to proclaim to. As Dr. Duryea forcibly put it, "The sick soul needs not a lecture on medicine, but a prescription." Has

not the ordinary method of the physician of souls
been that of a lecturer rather than of a prescriber? Is
this the proper, or the sensible way? This volume
advocates the methods of wise personal prescription
for the sick soul.[2]

General preaching has its place; but it is only a preliminary
in this work; the harvest must be handpicked.

A stationary foghorn has its value on a reef, or a
rocky shore, as a warning to those who approach the
point of danger. We must not say that this mode of
sounding an alarm has no value, but we cannot
suppose that a foghorn, however clear its sound or
well-worked its mechanism, can fill the place of a
coast guard of trained lifesavers, who are on the
watch to put out with their well-manned lifeboat to
save endangered single souls.[3]

The strongest preachers are unhesitating in their conviction
as to the primary importance of individual work.

As a rule, the intensity of the appeal is in inverse
proportion to the area covered; in other words, the
greater your audience, the smaller the probability of
your appeal coming home to a single heart. I once
heard Henry Ward Beecher say, "The longer I live,
the more confidence I have in those sermons
preached where one man is the minister and one
man is the congregation; where there's no question
as to who is meant when the preacher says, 'Thou
art the man.' " Years after this, I heard the Reverend Dr. Nevius speak similarly as to the missionary
field in China. He said he wanted no great preachers

in his field. That was not the sort of missionaries who were needed in China. If he could find a man who could talk familiarly, face-to-face, with another man, wherever he met him, he had missionary work for that kind of man in China. This is the way to do Christian work in China, or in America.

Such a man was Mr. Moody, who thought more of how many individual souls he could reach than of his preaching before any audience, however large, was always desirous of getting through with his preparatory pulpit appeal and of getting at his more important work of pleading with individual souls in the inquiry meeting. And that is the feeling of every earnest evangelist who thinks more of the work of reaping and harvesting than of the work of incessantly sowing broadcast seed that may, or that may not, have final fruitage.[4]

It is not merely that individual work is a helpful addition to other work of the minister, but that it is the chief work, and that from it come strength and power for other work.

And which would any sensible pastor and preacher choose for his church if it were merely a matter of choice: to have great revival meetings, or to have every church member actively and persistently engaged in individual soul-winning seven days in the week all the year round? The second would ensure the first; but the first, unfortunately, occurs without being followed by the second.

## Individual Work Christ's Preferred Method

Because this is the most effective way to win souls, it was Christ's preferred method; and because it was Christ's pre-ferred method, it is the most effective way. We are not told just how all the twelve disciples were won to Christ, but we are told how seven of them were. Peter, and Andrew, and James, and John, and Philip, and Nathanael, and Matthew were won to Christ by individual work. It is reasonable to believe that the method which is recorded with these seven was followed with some or all of the others. Christ proclaimed His message by preaching, as His ministers must do today; but Christ won men and women to the acceptance of His message and of Himself as Messiah and Savior by His loving, deeply personal, individual evangelism—conversational evangelism, it has been well-called.

Yet it is not surprising that the best method of soul-winning has not yet been as widely recognized as it deserves.

The superior effectiveness of this method of soul-winning is a matter of simple observation. We can test this ourselves, as we ask men how they were led to make the actual decision for Christ. After half a century's retrospect Dr. Trumbull wrote:

> The more extensive and varied has been my experience, and the more I have known of the Christian labors of others, the more positive is my conviction that the winning of one soul to Christ, or of ten thousand souls to Christ, is best done by the effort of an individual with an individual, not by the proclamation of an individual to a multitude, larger or smaller, without the accompanying or following face-to-face pleading with the single soul.
>
> This is my conviction today more positively than ever before. However others may feel about it, I cannot have a doubt on the subject. Winning one soul at a time usually results in the winning of a multitude of souls in the process of time. But addressing a multitude of souls, and urging them all to trust and serve Christ, may not be the means of winning even one soul to Christ, now or at any time.

## Its Effectiveness in Sunday School Work

Within a few weeks of my first entering Christ's service, I became the superintendent of a newly organized mission Sunday school in Hartford. In this, my first field of Christian work, I found that I could do most and best by appealing to the individual when he and I were alone together, rather than by my most effective appeals from the desk, or by my most attractive endeavors to impress the school as a whole. Occasionally, when a boy whose conduct and influence seemed hopelessly bad was not to be reached through anything said by teacher or superintendent in the presence of others, I found that a personal talk when no one else could see us would give me a hold on him, so that I could lead him to a better view, and a higher estimate, of his possibilities and duties. A good superintendent or a good teacher will often do more for Christ and for the most incorrigible pupil by a half hour's talk with that pupil all by himself out of the school than is done for such a person in a year's time by superintendent and teacher in the school or class as a whole.

## Its Effectiveness in College

More than thirty years ago, a group of clergymen were considering whether they should invite a well-known "evangelist" to conduct a series of "revival meetings" in the community. Some of these clergymen criticized the methods of work and the manner of this evangelist. Finally, a clergyman

who was something of a sacramentarian in his views
and practices, and therefore least likely to be in
sympathy with revival methods, surprised all
present by saying, earnestly:

"The public methods of this man, in his work, are
not what I prefer, but I was his fellow student in
college, and I knew him well there. In my own case,
I was a skeptic when I entered college, and I was not
interested in the subject of religion. But that man's
appeals I had to meet, and I could not resist them.
Because of his faithfulness, my life is given to the
Christian ministry. And now, though I may disagree
with that man's methods, I cannot but be grateful for
his personal devotion to Jesus Christ."

## Its Effectiveness in Politics

National politics was just then assuming more
importance as a great moral issue, in view of the
struggle over the extension of slavery into free
territory. It was about the time of the formation of
the Republican party. I was on the stump for the
first candidates of that party; and I was active in the
work of canvassing for the election of those candidates. In this field, as in the Sunday school field, I
found that the effective political work was to be
done, not in the public meetings, addressed by
eloquent speakers, but in the quiet, systematic
searching out of the individual voter and winning
him to the right side. Indeed, I had the privilege of
introducing and advocating measures for an extension of this canvassing for individual voters which
were novel then, but which gained in recognition

and prominence as their superior effectiveness was evidenced. No political campaign is won by speakers on the stump. Stump speeches arouse enthusiasm and make voters ready to work; but the campaign is won by the man-to-man canvass of the individual voter. One man is more than a hundred in the field of missions or of politics. Until that thought prevails, the world will never be won to Christ, or to any good cause.

## Its Effectiveness in Every Field

After my return from the army I was again in the Sunday school missionary field, which I had left to go out as a chaplain. For ten years I addressed gatherings of persons in numbers from ten or fifteen to five or six thousand each. In this work I went from Maine to California, and from Minnesota to Florida. This gave me an opportunity to test the relative value of speeches to gathered assemblies. Later, I have been for more than twenty-five years an editor of a religious periodical that has had a circulation of more than a hundred thousand a week during much of the time. Meanwhile I have published more than thirty different volumes. Yet looking back upon my work, in all these years, I can see more direct results of good through my individual efforts with individuals, than I can know of through all my spoken words to thousands upon thousands of persons in religious assemblies, or all my written words on the pages of periodicals or of books. And in this I do not think that my experience has been wholly unlike that of many others who have had large experience in both spheres of influence.

Reaching one person at a time is the best way of reaching all the world in time. Reaching one person at a time is the best way of reaching a single individual. The world is made up of individuals. Christ longs for individuals to be in his service. Therefore he who considers Christ's love, or the world's needs, will think most of individuals, and will do most for individuals.[5]

Many of Christ's followers do not realize that they themselves were won by an individual word until they stop to recall what it was that finally threw the balance in favor of their open confession of Christ. Sermons, general evangelistic appeals, home training, an impressive book, Sunday school influence, may all prepare the way, but the matter is seldom closed without the individual word to the individual. The writer, brought up in a Christian home and Sunday school, did not realize that this was so in his own case until comparatively recently, when he asked himself just what led to the final decision, as a boy of thirteen, to confess his Lord openly as Savior. Then it came back to him. It was the word of a playmate, a little younger than himself, who said to him one day, as they talked together: "Father says that Jesus said that whoever would confess him before men, he would confess before the Father in heaven, and whoever denied him before men, he would deny before the Father in heaven. I don't want him to deny me, and I'm going to join the church next communion Sunday." It was not, perhaps, meant as an invitation; it was only a boyish but manly statement of what he was going to do, and why he was going to do it. But the *reason* had never before been made so plain and convincing to the other boy, who went home to talk it over with his parents; and at the next opportunity those two lads stood up together in their home church to confess before men their Savior, going out together from that service, one to be called to his Savior only three years later, the other to thank God many years afterward for the fidelity of the friend who won him to Christ.

## Individual Work the Hardest Work

Individual soul-winning is not easy work. It is hard. It is the hardest work that God asks us to do for Him. Before trying to reason out why, or to argue that the simple extending to a fellowman of an invitation to share with us the richest joy of our life *ought* to be an easy thing to do, let us frankly admit that it is hard, and face that fact to begin with.

Even those whose professional and only life business is soul-saving find it difficult. Ask any minister friend which is easier for him to do: to preach a sermon, or to seek an opportunity to talk alone with an individual about that one's spiritual welfare.

Many a man who is eloquent before a large congregation is dumb before a single individual. Bossuet, the great French preacher, said frankly as to this very matter: "It requires more faith and courage to say two words face-to-face with one single sinner, than from the pulpit to rebuke two or three thousand persons, ready to listen to everything, on condition of forgetting all."[6]

## Will It Grow Easy?

If it is so hard even for the trained minister, it is not to be expected that laymen will do it more easily. But if it is our greatest work, and if it is Christ's preferred method because it is the most effective method, will this work grow easy as we go on in its accomplishment? Will long-continued practice bring ease and facility?

Probably not. If it "takes it out" of a man to sell goods, or write life insurance, or solicit advertising, or do anything else that means bringing another across from his position to ours, is there anything we ought to be more sharply watchful against in ourselves than slipping into a superficial "facility" in soul-winning? We not only must not expect the work to grow easy, but we must realize that if it does so, something is wrong.

Dr. Trumbull was often spoken of as being a man of exceptional "tact." He practiced individual soul-winning pretty constantly from the time when he first found his Savior, at twenty-one, until his death more than fifty years later. People who knew him and his ways, and his lifelong habit, have said of him, "Oh, it was 'second nature' to Dr. Trumbull to speak to a man about his soul. He fairly couldn't help doing it, it was so easy for him. I never could get his ease in the work." And in so saying they showed how little they knew of him or of the demands of this work upon every man.

The book on *Individual Work* was written after its author was seventy years of age. Hear what he had to say as to the "ease" which his long practice had brought him:

> From nearly half a century of such practice, I can say that I have spoken with thousands upon thousands on the subject of their spiritual welfare. Yet, I find it as difficult to speak about it at the end of these years as at the beginning. Never to the present day can I speak to a single soul for Christ without being reminded by Satan that I am in danger of harming the cause by introducing it just now. If there is one thing that Satan is sensitive

> about, it is the danger of a Christian's harming the
> cause he loves by speaking of Christ to a needy
> soul. He [Satan] has more than once, or twice, or
> thrice, kept me from speaking on the subject by his
> sensitive pious caution, and he has tried a thousand
> times to do so. Therefore my experience leads me
> to suppose that he is urging other persons to try any
> method for souls except the best one.[7]

This work is the hardest work in the world simply because it *is* the most effective work for Christ. The devil strikes hardest and most persistently at the forces which will, if effective, hurt his cause most. He devotes his chief energies to those from whom he has most to fear; their sides he never leaves. Therefore the worker who seeks to win individuals to Christ may rest assured that he has, by entering upon that work, served notice upon the devil for a life-and-death conflict; and that notice will be accepted by the devil as an obligation to swerve the worker from his purpose whenever, by any subtle means in the devil's power, this can be done. Let us write in large letters in our mental or real notebooks the devil's favorite argument.

> His favorite argument with a believer is that just
> now is not a good time to speak on the subject. The
> lover of Christ and of souls is told that he will harm
> the cause he loves by introducing the theme of
> themes just now.[8]

This, then, is what we face when we enter upon this work. It is the greatest and hardest work in the world; it will never grow easy, but it will never grow small. If it always remains the hardest, it always remains also the greatest. There will seldom be an opportunity free from some strong reason why we should "do it later." But the devil is back of the reason.

## Questions for Study and Discussion

1. In what senses and passages is the verb "take alive" used in the New Testament?
2. What three facts may be asserted concerning individual work?
3. Does a minister's professional position give him any distinctive advantage for the doing of individual work? Give your reasons.
4. For what reasons would you say individual soul-winning is the greatest work in the world?
5. What was Dr. Duryea's comment on the need of a sick soul?
6. Mention any preacher's statement as to the need of individual work, or his example in its doing.
7. What striking fact in Christ's ministry shows what importance He attached to the work?
8. Why are less effective methods of Christian service likely to be heard from more than this most effective method of all?
9. Describe any striking instances of individual soul-winning you have known of personally, either in your own or in others' experiences, and apart from the cases mentioned in this book.
10. How does the principle of working with individuals apply in every field?
11. Consider carefully whether your own actual and final decision to accept Christ as your Savior was induced by the word of an individual to you as an individual. If it was, describe the circumstances and the impression made upon you at the time.
12. Have you ever known anyone who claimed that it was, as a rule, easy for him to do individual work? If so, what characteristics in his work do you notice?
13. Why is individual soul-winning likely to be hard work? Why ought it to be hard?

# The Worker and His Equipment

## Questions to Ask Yourself Before You Read the Chapter

1. What would you say is the best equipment for successful individual soul-winning?
2. Of what should one make sure before attempting individual work?
3. Under what circumstances might one properly refrain from speaking to another on the subject of personal religion?
4. Are there dangers in this work? What are they?
5. Of what mistake should we be most afraid?
6. Can one who is conscious of personal defects and shortcomings properly undertake the work?
7. How is equipment best to be gained?

# 2
# The Worker and His Equipment

Is there any need to ask, now, who should do individual work? Can any follower of Christ accept Christ's offer of salvation for himself and refuse to pass it on? Layman or minister, Christ knows no distinctions here, makes no exceptions in His Commission to His followers. It is every layman's chief work, without which every other business and accomplishment of life counts as nothing, but added to which, ordinary or extraordinary occupations are tenfolded in value and effectiveness. It is every minister's chief work, without which pulpit and other labors are empty of life-bringing power, but added to which all his labors teem with life and love that are irresistible.

But what do we need before we begin? How must we be prepared? What brings effectiveness? Shall we wait until we have an expert knowledge of the Bible? Of theology? Power in argument? Skill in discussion?

To get a decisive answer to these questions, stop and consider what "individual work" is. It is simply telling others of our experience of Christ's love, so that they may share it. This does not call first for an expert knowledge of the contents of the Bible, or of theology, or for skill in discussion

and power in argument. It *does* call for unshaken, unshakable
knowledge of what Jesus Christ has done for us, and for a
deeply rooted purpose to share that knowledge with others.
That is all. We must know Christ, and we must know the
one to whom we would make Christ attractive. There are
certain ways which are more likely than others to win persons
to us, and those ways it is the purpose of this book to study.
But we need not hold off from the work even for this brief
study. The best way to begin is to begin; and the best time to
begin is now.

> The real question is not, "Is this the best time for
> a personal word for Christ?" but it is "Am I willing
> to improve this time for Christ?" If the Christian
> waits until the sinner gives sign of a desire for help,
> or until the Christian thinks that a loving word to
> the sinner will be most timely, he is not likely to
> begin at all. The only safe rule for his guidance—if
> indeed a Christian needs a specific rule as a guide—
> is to speak lovingly of Christ and of Christ's love for
> the individual whenever one has an opportunity of
> choosing his subject of conversation in an interview
> with an individual who may be in special need, yet
> who has given no special indication of it. This
> seems to have been Paul's idea in his counsel to
> young Timothy: "Preach the word; be instant in
> season, out of season; reprove, rebuke, exhort, with
> all longsuffering and doctrine." The most important
> of all themes of converse would seem to be worthy
> of prominence in comparison with others.[1]

Of course, this does not mean that one is to engage in this
most subtle and vital work in a haphazard, indiscriminate way,

without any reference to one's surroundings or acquaintance-ship. Dr. Trumbull illustrated this principle with the follow-ing story:

> Mr. Studd and some of his Cambridge associates came to me, after a meeting, and asked my assistance in behalf of one of their countrymen who was with them. He was a young man standing high in his university. His father was eminent in the nation. Hence the influence of the young man would be great according to he used it for or against the right. He had, as yet, no interest in Christianity.
>
> "Give us your help, Dr. Trumbull," said Mr. Studd. "It would amply repay us for coming to America if we could only win this man to Christ."
>
> "My dear friends," I said, "I cannot help you. I have no special power in winning souls. I have merely told you this evening of my habit of speaking a word for Christ to those whom God puts under my influence, or for whom, in some way, he gives me a responsibility. This young man is not one of that sort. I have merely met him here as one with you. All I can say is that I will have your request in mind, and if I meet him so that I have a right to speak to him I will not fail to use the opportunity."
>
> "Well, we shall be praying for you and him, and I trust that God will open a way for a blessing."
>
> It was then nearly midnight. I left the Auditorium and went across the campus to the hall in which I had my room. As I went up the steps of that hall I saw a young man standing in the shadow. He stepped forward to meet me. It was the young Cambridge student of whom we had been speaking,

and for whom his friends and associates were now praying. As I greeted him cordially, he said:

"Dr. Trumbull, I was over in the Auditorium and I heard your address. And now I want your help. When are you going away? When can I have a talk with you?"

It was arranged that I should meet him after breakfast the next morning. Bidding him good night, I went to my room to thank God and to pray to God. As I came from the breakfast room I found him awaiting me. Together we sought a retired spot, under the trees, at some distance from the buildings. There we had a plain, free talk. He was entirely ready to take the step of submission to Christ, and of entering His service. As we kneeled together in the open air, and sought God's blessing on the decision then made and the new life course then entered on, I felt that the incident was one of God's planning and leading to, and which surely had His blessing.

I was glad to report to those who had sought my help this sequel to their request of the evening before. And when I left them all, that noon, I was confident that the new disciple would be lovingly and faithfully cared for and aided in the subsequent days at Northfield and when all returned to their English homes. Some weeks later I had a letter from that young man, speaking most gratefully of that interview under the trees on that morning in Northfield—that "heaven on earth," as he called it, and as any place where God is can fairly be called. God is always better than we anticipate, if we are ready to work for souls in His behalf.[2]

## What Mistakes Shall We Fear?

A prominent preacher once sent to Dr. Trumbull, for publication in *The Sunday School Times*, an article on "The Dangers of Personal Evangelism." It was returned to its author unpublished. For Dr. Trumbull had learned early in his work that there is only one mistake to be really afraid of here. Of a certain experience he wrote:

That experience with my first young convert in the army encouraged me in my individual work with individuals there. I saw that it were better to make a mistake in one's first effort at a personal religious conversation, and correct that mistake afterwards, than not to make any effort. There can be no mistake so bad, in working for an individual soul for Christ, as the fatal mistake of not making any honest endeavor. How many persons refrain from doing anything lest they should possibly do the wrong thing just now! Not doing is the worst of doing.[3]

The army experience in which he at first feared he had done harm was the following:

My first experience under fire was on a winter Sunday in eastern North Carolina. We had bivouacked for the night in an open field, when starting on a raid into the enemy's country. As we rose in the early morning to make ready for a march, the blazing camp fires on every side, throwing their lurid light on the stacked arms, and the moving soldiers, with the hum of conflicting voices, made a weird and impressive scene; and as I heard for the first time the command, to a company near where I stood, "Load at will," followed by the ring of the rammers in the steel rifle barrels driving home the cartridges, I was thrilled by the sounds as never before. Realizing, as I did, that when those rifles were discharged it would be in deadly conflict, and that before the day should close some of the brave men near me would probably be in the presence of their Maker, I had a sense of responsibility for souls as never before, yet as often afterwards.

Moving about among the fire-lit groups, and looking for a man standing by himself, I came upon a soldier, a bright Connecticut boy, with whom I had often spoken in camp. He was arranging his belt at the moment. I spoke to him cheerily of the activities of the hour, and of the possibilities of the coming day. Then I asked him tenderly if he had committed himself trustfully to his Savior.

"Ah, Chaplain! This is no time to think of such things. It would unfit me for a fight if I got to thinking about myself just now."

"It is always a time, Sergeant, for thinking about Him who is able to care for us in every hour of life or of death, and who loves us more than we can ever love Him. But if you don't want to talk about this now I shall come to you when we are back in camp, if we get there together once more; and then, certainly, I can have a good talk with you about this matter, for I want you to do your duty."

Our raid was a successful one, and soon we were back in camp once more. I looked up my young sergeant friend, and told him that I had come to renew our conversation of the morning after our first night's bivouac, on the recent raid. I had a plain, earnest talk with him. He promised to go, in need and trust, to his Savior, and commit himself to Him for life and death. After a while, when we were in St. Augustine, we organized a regimental church, and this young sergeant was the first one to stand up and make a confession of his Savior.[4]

After a meeting at which I had been urging the duty of being willing to risk mistakes rather than make the greatest mistake of saying nothing for Christ, a woman present told of her experience. She had longed to lead to Christ a girl in her Sunday school class. One day she called upon the girl, determined to have a loving talk about the matter. But her courage failed; she talked about every subject but the greatest one, and when she left, the purpose of her call had not been mentioned. She started home in discouragement, wheeled around, went back to the house, and in a blundering, faltering way she told her young friend how she wished she would give herself to the Savior. Then the teacher left the house for the second time and went home, but not before the girl had plainly shown that she was very angry at her caller for what she had dared to do. At the next communion service of the church that young girl stood up and, confessing Christ as her Savior, was received into full membership in the church. Her teacher went to her with a full heart, told her how glad she was, and asked her what it was that had led her to take the step. "Why, it was what you said to me that day you called," was the reply. And one Sunday school teacher rejoiced that she had dared to make a "mistake."

## Our Feelings and Our Defects

Our "feelings" have no place as a factor in this work. What is called "the passion for souls" would seem to be a feeling of overwhelming desire to win others to Christ that very few possess or ever will possess. But that absence of feeling neither relieves us of our simple duty nor need hinder us in its doing. We do not have to like one before seeking to win him to Christ. If we saw a neighbor's house on fire, we should not stop to weigh our feelings for that neighbor before sounding the alarm. Feelings will seldom lead one to the doing of this supreme duty. But both love and liking for a fellowman are very likely to follow our unselfish efforts to bring this greatest of blessings to him. Our constant effort in the Christian life ought to be to get the better of our feelings, and not to let our feelings get the better of us.

What of the worker's own character, or lack of character, as bearing on the doing of this work? Shall we let the consciousness of our own unworthiness, our many shortcomings, keep us from it? Shall we hold off until our own lives are more nearly in accord with the Christ-life, better examples of what Christ can do for one?

Why should we? Is not our own unworthiness, after all, one of the chief appeals that we can make to those who are like us in this terrible need of a Savior? We speak as *saved sinners*, not as superior beings. We *know* whereof we speak, for we know the need, and we know how great is the saving love that can outweigh even our unworthiness. That love of Christ we would share, for all need it even as we do. "For we preach not ourselves, but Christ Jesus the Lord; and ourselves your servants for Jesus' sake. . . . But we have this treasure in earthen vessels, that the excellency of the power may be of God, and not of us" (2 Corinthians 4:5, 7).

It is not so much a question of our defects as of Christ's sufficiency, or of the difficulty in the way of speaking as of our purpose to overcome such difficulty. A pathetically striking instance of determination to speak for Christ to individuals is given in S. H. Hadley's account of Jerry McAuley's first efforts. While in prison Jerry had been won to his Savior.

> He immediately went to work with an ardor and courage that would put many of us missionaries to shame. Under the rules of the prison at that time, very little opportunity was given to speak to any one. Only as they were marching to and fro, with lockstep, from prison to workshop, from workshop to meals, and then back to prison again, could he speak to the man in front and the one behind, telling the burning news that was filling his soul, that he had found Jesus, that his sins were pardoned, and how happy he was in his new-found joy.
> At the table he was able to speak to the one on his right hand, and the one on his left, but even with this limited opportunity a wonderful revival broke out in the prison as a result of Jerry's labors. Missionaries of the city went up, and every opportunity was given them by the management. Bible classes were formed of the converts, and wonderful work was done for God. Jerry was the center of all this activity.[5]

Of this we may be sure: Nothing brings into one's own life such a powerful lift to higher levels as the doing of individual work for others. It is bound to raise one's own standards of life and conduct. It is the most effective safeguard against personal failure that we can ever find. The best way to conquer self is to forget self in an effort to help "the other fellow."

Not only will continued work in this field strengthen our spiritual fiber and deepen our spiritual life, but it will inevitably lead us into more thoughtful and profitable Bible study, broaden our other interests, increase our sensitiveness and tact, and give us ever greater power to love. Yet all these blessings to self will come only from a complete forgetting of self in our loving interest in others.

## Our Right to Be Confident

Finally, as to the confidence with which we enter upon this work. If it is the greatest work to which God calls us every one, can we be in any doubt as to its having His blessing? There is no room here for self-confidence; but there is no room, either, for lack of God-confidence. We have the same Power working with us that Jesus had with Him. ". . . as my Father hath sent me," He says to His disciples, "even so send I you" (John 20:21). Results we shall not always see. But results we must always hope for and believe in. "You don't expect to have conversions every time you preach, do you?" Spurgeon is said to have asked a young minister who was seeking how to get greater results from his ministry. "Oh, no," said the young man. "Then you won't," was the retort.

## Questions for Study and Discussion

1. Why are none exempt from the obligation to do individual soul-winning?
2. What effect has the doing of this work upon one's other occupations?
3. What is individual work, simply defined?
4. What is not called for, in the way of equipment? What is called for?
5. What two persons must we know in order to do the work well?
6. How would you draw the line between haphazard, indiscriminate working, and that which is not?
7. What is the only mistake that need really be feared?
8. Have you ever known personally of an instance where the worker feared that a mistake had been made, yet which resulted well? Describe it.
9. What place have our feelings in this work? Why?
10. Should a person who is conscious of failures in his own life attempt this work? Why?
11. What is the effect of this work upon oneself?
12. Give two strong reasons why we should have confidence as we enter upon the work.

# Need of a
# Life-Resolve

## Questions to Ask Yourself Before You Read the Chapter

1. What do you think, in general, of the wisdom of making pledges, or resolutions?
2. Has anyone a right to expect Christ to pledge Himself to save him, who is unwilling to pledge himself, in turn, to serve Christ faithfully? Is this a fair way to look at the pledge question?
3. What statement did you make or give assent to when you united with the church (this can be obtained from your pastor)? Study this, and ascertain its bearing on your obligation to do individual work. Is it equivalent to a pledge to do this work?
4. Frame a simple form of pledge or resolution to make a practice of individual soul-winning.
5. What gain would there be in the definite, prayerful making of such a resolution?

# 3
# Need of a Life-Resolve

HENRY Clay Trumbull was brought up in a home where exceptionally high standards prevailed, where both parents were earnest Christians. Yet, he passed through boyhood and out of his teens without having made any definite confession of Christ as his Savior.

He left his home in Stonington, Connecticut, to take a clerkship in a Hartford railroad office. About that time there was a religious revival, both in Stonington and Hartford, with special meetings in the latter city under the leadership of evangelist Charles Finney.

> But as I was boarding at a house where the young men at the table had only words of contempt or ridicule for the whole matter, I attended none of the meetings, did not at the first hear Mr. Finney, and had no conscious interest in his work or its results.[1]

Before he left Stonington, one of his most intimate friends there had taken the stand for Christ, and so had others. But no one had a word to say on the subject to young Trumbull.

Had any one of them, or had anyone else, spoken
a personal word to me at that time, I would have
welcomed it gladly; but no such word came.

I was, indeed, somewhat surprised that my friend
had no word to say on the subject, then or at some
time later, intimate as he and I were. Especially
was this the case as we corresponded freely during
his college course in Yale. When I was about
twenty-one years old I removed to Hartford, and I
continued to correspond freely with my Stonington
friend.[2]

What followed came, therefore, with the more unexpectedness.

One noon, as I was returning from my midday
meal, I stopped at the post office for the noon mail.
A letter came from my Stonington friend. This
surprised me, for I had not yet acknowledged his
letter of a few days before. As I read the first few
lines of the letter, I saw that it was a personal appeal
to me. At once crumpling the letter in my hand I
thrust it into my pocket, saying to a friend who was
with me, "I think there must be a big revival in
Stonington, if it has set my old friend preaching to
me." Then, brushing the subject away from my
mind, I started down Asylum Street toward my
office and my work.

But the subject of that letter, and the letter itself,
would not stay brushed away. I asked myself how it
was that that letter, on that subject, had been
written. In all our years of intimacy since my friend
had come out openly for Christ, he had never

before said or written a word on this subject. Had it
been an easy thing for him to do now? Was it a
desire for his own enjoyment, or a desire for my
good, that had prompted this writing? It was worthwhile to read that letter, and consider its contents,
before throwing it aside permanently. These were
the thoughts that naturally ran in my mind as I
walked toward my office.

The office of the chief engineer, where my work
lay, was on the third floor of one of the stone towers
of the railroad station. Instead of stopping in that
office, where I usually stopped, I passed through it,
and went into a little map closet on that upper floor.
Shutting myself into the map closet, where I could
be entirely alone, I took out from my pocket the
crumpled letter, smoothed it out, and began with
real interest to read.[3]

The letter was an earnest appeal from one man, who had
found the Savior, to another who did not yet know that joy. It
opened with a half apology for the seeming "intrusion," went
on to explain how hard it had been to write on this subject,
added "I may never have the courage to address you again in
this matter," and closed with the earnest hope that the reader
would therefore "be advised by me now."

Before I had read the last of this letter, I was on
my knees in that corner map room in that lofty
tower summit, asking forgiveness of God, and
committing myself to a long slighted Savior. That
was a turning point in my life course; and in a half
century that has passed since then I have been
renewedly more and more grateful for the writing of

that letter, and for the loving spirit that prompted
it. And I have wished that other friends were as true
to their friends.[4]

The lesson of the need of the individual effort for souls was
just beginning to take root in this man's life, as it was the start
of his own new life.

So soon as I had come to the point of Christian
decision for myself, I looked about me for another
man. I did not have far to go. An associate with me
in the office of the chief engineer was a fellow
boarder with me in the house which was my
temporary home. We were accustomed to walk
together to and from the boardinghouse and the
office. We were near each other all day in the
office, and we sat near each other at the boardinghouse table. As we walked together from the
house to the office, I told my friend of my new
decision for Christ, and I urged him to make a like
decision.[5]

Here was the answer that burned in the lesson so deep:

"Trumbull, your words cut me to the heart. You
little think how they rebuke me. I've long been a
professed follower of Christ; and you have never
suspected this, although we've been in close association in house and office for years. I've never said
a word to you for the Savior whom I trust. I've
never urged you to trust Him. I've never said a
word for Him. And now a follower of His, and a
friend of yours, from a distance, has been the

means of leading you to Him. And here you are,
inviting me to come to that Savior of whom I have
been a silent follower for years. May God forgive
me for my lack of faithfulness!"[6]

Is it surprising that those two incidents in Christian work,
one bringing him into eternal life, the other revealing the
careless neglect of the greatest matter in the world so common
among Christian people, had an effect on this man that he
determined, God helping him, he would never outgrow? The
effect was deliberately crystallized in this way:

Then it was that I made a purpose and resolve
for life. The purpose I formed was, as an
imperative duty, not to fail in my Christian life in
the particular way that these two friends of mine
confessed that they had consciously failed. I
determined that as I loved Christ, and as Christ
loved souls, I would press Christ on the individual
soul, so that none who were in the proper sphere
of my individual responsibility or influence should
lack the opportunity of meeting the question
whether or not they would individually trust and
follow Christ. The resolve I made was that,
whenever I was in such intimacy with a soul as to
be justified in choosing my subject of conversation,
the theme of themes should have prominence
between us, so that I might learn his need, and, if
possible, meet it.[7]

There was the life-resolve that shaped and controlled that
life during the more than fifty years that followed its prayerful
making. Is it a resolve that any disciple of Christ ought to

hesitate to make? Is to do so anything more than the meeting
of our simplest duty as Christ's loyal followers? But could
anything bring a greater blessing, a richer harvest of souls,
into the Kingdom today, than the making and keeping of this
resolve by Christian people generally? Here is the resolution
that we are facing:

> Whenever I am justified in choosing my subject
> of conversation with another, the theme of themes
> shall have prominence between us, so that I may
> learn his need, and, if possible, meet it.

## Questions for Study and Discussion

1. Why does it not necessarily follow that the influences
   of a Christian home, and of church and Sunday
   school training, always result in one's accepting
   Christ as Savior?
2. What commonly surprises non-Christians about the
   attitude of their Christian friends?
3. Why is it that a large number of people in any
   community are always unreached by revival meetings?
4. How may revival meetings be given greatest effectiveness?
5. What incident made a profound impression on
   H. Clay Trumbull just after he had been won to
   Christ by an individual appeal?

6. Do you think that that experience, in his first attempt at soul-winning, might be duplicated in a good many cases today, or not?

7. What was the life-resolve that the young convert made?

8. Analyze that resolve, showing how it guards against haphazard or discourteous effort, under what circumstances it calls for the doing of the work, why the resolve ought to be made, and what is its definite and declared purpose.

# Winning at the Start

## Questions to Ask Yourself Before You Read the Chapter

1. State the ultimate purpose of the work in which we are seeking to gain proficiency.
2. Why, should you say, does much depend upon the way in which we approach a person?
3. What should we try to accomplish in our approach?
4. What is the best kind of approach to make?
5. What is the worst kind of approach to make?
6. Give your own definition of tact.
7. What place has tact in this work? Why?
8. Was Jesus tactful? Can you give any illustrations of His tact?
9. What place has personal criticism in this work?
10. Mention two or three sure ways to win people to us.

# 4
# Winning at the Start

WHEN we are face-to-face with an opportunity, which means face-to-face with one whom we would win to Christ, how shall we begin? *What shall we be thinking most about as we prepare to come into close quarters?* Shall we be hunting in our memory for a Bible text to quote? Shall we be running over in our mental notebook the various groups or classifications of "cases," so that we may decide in which pigeonhole this "case" belongs? Shall we try to remember how this or that noted soul-winner worked?

If we concentrate on any of these lines at the moment of beginning, we shall be missing the most important factor in the situation. When a man is fishing with rod and line and fly, and is about to cast, what holds his chief attention then, and from then on? It is the *fish*, is it not? When a man is after game in the woods, and is about to attempt to bring his game down, what is the one thing in the world on which his eyes and thoughts and interests are riveted? *The game itself.* He must forget everything else in an absorbed, alert watching of the animal and its every movement. He must *know* his game, and its interests, if he would capture it.

If we would take a man alive for Christ, we must first of all know something, be it ever so little, about that man and his present interests. Our knowledge may be gained in ten

seconds; again, it may take ten months to gain. But we can
never have this needed knowledge of the man, as a first step
toward winning the man himself, unless we devote our whole
energy, for the time being, to knowing the man. Therefore it
is *he* that must fill our whole horizon as we prepare to come
into close quarters with him. We must be thinking not about
*others*, but about *this other;* just this one in the whole universe.

This is the simple secret of "tact"—that mysterious power
which a few favored ones seem to possess, and which, if one
does not happen to have the "gift," is regretfully supposed to
be beyond one's reach. But "tact" is simply "touch": a touch
on the right spot rather than the wrong; a touch that will win
another, rather than antagonize him; a touch in keeping with,
rather than opposed to, his present interests. And it is
impossible to touch one at a point that will interest him unless
we know something of what his interests are. The art of
taking men alive calls for tact at the very beginning, which
means, first of all, studying your man.

This concentrating all our attention on the individual at the
outset, so that we may know what interests him, is to enable
us to put forward something that shall attract and hold his
attention.

For let us bear in mind that we are in the business of
*winning* men to Christ. We cannot win by antagonizing. And
we must win by drawing men to *us*, as a first step in drawing
them to Christ.

## The Other Man's Interests as Bait

It is the other man's interests, just where they are, and as
they are, not as we think or know they ought to be, that we
must recognize and work with. We cannot expect others to

cross over from their interests to ours until we have first crossed over from our interests to theirs.

The Master Fisherman has given us a striking instance of the use of this bait-principle in the record of the training of some of His first disciples.

He had the whole world to choose from when He began the special training of the few men with whom He was to entrust the continuance of the winning of the world to Himself. Several of these chosen few were fishermen. That was not an accident, nor was their fishing a mere incident in their previous life. The principles of successful fishing were already dominant factors in their lives. And one of their earliest lessons in soul-winning was taught through a miraculous fishing experience that Jesus gave them. Still more clearly, there was no accident in this.

Even the Son of God did not take it for granted that men would be interested in Him or His message until He had first interested Himself in them. Shall we expect to do better than He? If not, we must be willing to work as He did. Let us watch Him at work on the lakeside (Luke 5:1–11).

He is teaching the eager multitude the Word of God. But, always more interested in the individual than in the crowd, He is watching some fishermen nearby whom He knows and whom He has been trying to awaken to a sense of His mission, and to the need of taking part in it. So He asks one of them to help by permitting the use of his boat as a pulpit; and then He goes on with His message to the multitude.

With what indication of response or interest from the fishermen? None at all. The reason is plain enough. They had had a profitless, exhausting night of it in their trade. A fisherman does not mind getting tired out by hard work if he has a boatload of fish to show for his efforts. But to work all night and take nothing! The physical exhaustion then is doubled by the discouragement. And the nets have to be cleaned, too, just as though the catch had been a big one! Washing nets, at its best, is pretty dull business; but washing nets that have stayed empty all night is enough to take the heart out of any man.

It was a cheerless, discouraging day that was just breaking for those tired men by the sea. What if a great teacher *was* expounding precious spiritual truth within earshot? Human nature wanted none of that—just then. Could any human being fairly have been expected to be interested in spiritual matters under those circumstances?

Jesus knew how it was. It did not call for His supernatural insight into "what was in man" to appreciate that the men He was trying to train were more interested in the fish they had failed to catch that morning than in anything else in the universe.

Yet this fact, instead of making Him impatient, or deterring Him from any attempt to go on with their training, was to Him a challenge, an invitation. It was His opportunity to use tact, to use bait. He must touch them at the point of their present interests, unworthy though these interests might seem in comparison with higher spiritual matters. He must use a bait that would attract these men just as they were, without waiting until they should come, of their own accord, to worthier interests.

Fish—the fish they hadn't caught—were their present interest. Fish, then, must be the bait. So His first word to them is, "Put out into the deep, and let down your nets for a catch." They protested, of course.

But because His very manner showed them that He was intent on giving their own temporal interests His supreme attention, they yielded. And then, after He had given them such proof of His genuine interest in them as they never forgot, and they had taken care of the nets that were breaking and the boats that were sinking from the draught of fishes which *He* had helped them to catch, they were ready to think of other things than fish. They were ready, then, to be interested in *anything* that Jesus had to offer, because He had first interested Himself in them.

Now, and not until now, can Christ hope for a response as He says, in effect: "I have helped you to catch fish; I want you to help me to catch men. From now on you will take men alive."

It is so easy to miss the principles of Christ's methods of soul-winning if we will not look for them. One of the most prominent commentators of this generation has actually written, of this incident: "There was absolutely no purpose, either of demonstration of Christ's mission or of help to human needs, to be served by the miracle. Its only significance is symbolical." But is it, indeed, either necessary or reasonable to suppose that the Master turned aside from His spiritual teaching and caused the miraculous draught of fishes simply in order that He might have a good illustration of what He wanted these disciples to take up as their lifework? They were already fishermen; He could easily have said to them, with their nets empty, "from now on you will take men alive," and they would have understood Him. But the empty nets would effectually have killed their interest in the invitation.

They were not interested in taking men alive then; they were absorbingly interested in catching fish. To be sure, this was not nearly so worthy an interest as the saving of men's souls; but Christ took men as they were, not as He would have liked them to be.

How differently most of us would have handled that situation! How we should have stormed and protested and argued with those men, indignantly urging them to forget their fish for a few minutes and turn their attention to something worthwhile! How surprised or hurt or discouraged we have been, in our own experiences, because those upon whom we have urged the blessings of life in Christ are obviously and persistently more interested in the unworthy affairs of this unworthy world! Have we ever given ourselves in any absorbing way to a study of what we are pleased to consider their "unworthy" interests, in order to be of genuine service to them? If we have not, we are failing in a first principle of the art upon which depends our success in the Great Commission.

## The Bait of Honest Commendation

We cannot do today just as Christ did by the lakeside—work a miracle to win men's interest. But there is another kind of bait that is within the reach of us all, and that calls for no miracle to use. It is a bait that Jesus Himself used freely in His soul-winning. This is the bait of *honest commendation*. It will land the most slippery human fish alive. No man can resist it. A word, heartily spoken, of sincere commendation for a fellow being, will disarm opposition and draw him to us more effectively than any other method. It is the best human bait in the world.

Perhaps one reason why honest commendation is so effective in challenging a person's interest is because it is so rare. A friend of mine, passing through a town on his travels, saw an old, gray-haired black man hard at work in the roadway. He greeted him pleasantly:

"That's a good piece of work you're doing."

The old man stopped, straightened up, looked the other over, then said slowly:

"Say, you don't live in this town, do you?"

"No, why?" asked the visitor.

"I been working here twenty years, and you're the first man who ever told me anything like that."

"But," says someone, "that's all well enough with a person whom you *can* commend, but suppose you are working with one whom you can *not* commend?" Wait a moment! Say that again! "One whom you can not commend?" That person does not live. If we think that we have ever met such a one, the fault is with ourselves, not with the seemingly unlovely person.

## Commending a Whiskey Drinker

An illustration of the possibility and the gain of using honest commendation at the outset with one whose confidence we would win is found in a railroad train experience resulting from such an opportunity as might come to any traveler.

> Entering, one November morning, at the Grand Central Station in New York, a crowded train for Boston, I found the only vacant seat was one alongside of a pleasant-faced, florid-complexioned, large-framed young man, and that seat I took, and began to read the morning paper. After a few minutes my seatmate took from his valise a large flask of whiskey and a metal drinking cup. Before drinking himself, he proffered it to me. As I thanked him and declined it, he drank by himself.[1]

Not a particularly hopeful outlook for soul-winning, most of us would feel, and still less did there seem to be any chance for commendation. But the fisherman was doing all that he could do as yet, by studying his man and holding himself in readiness.

> I still read my paper, but I thought of my seatmate, and I watched for an opportunity. In a little while he again turned to his valise, and, as before, took out his whiskey bottle. Once more he offered it to me, and again I declined it with thanks. As he put away the bottle, after drinking from it the second time, he said:
>
> "Don't you ever drink, my friend?"
>
> "No, my friend, I do not."
>
> "Well, I guess you think I'm a pretty rough fellow."[2]

Perhaps some of us would have already pointed out the danger and the wrong of his drinking. Or if not, we might have felt that he himself had now made the opening for a word of honest reproof. Surely there was no opportunity to commend anything in this whiskey-drinking stranger. But Dr. Trumbull had learned the first principle of man-fishing, and here was his friendly, honest answer, based on the one admirable quality in this man that loving penetration had discovered:

> "I think you're a very generous fellow."

Soon the young man was telling his life story:

> He was a Massachusetts country boy, now a clerk in a large New York jobbing house. He was just going to his old country home to spend Thanksgiv-

ing. He confessed that he had fallen into bad ways in the city, very different ways from those of his boyhood in Massachusetts. I asked him about his mother, and he spoke lovingly and tenderly of her. He said he knew she was praying for him constantly. This brought us into close quarters. I told him that I was sure his mother would be happy if he prayed for himself, and that he knew that he ought to do this. I urged him to do it.

He was evidently surprised and touched by my expressions of interest in him.

"Wouldn't you like to make your old mother happy, as you go home to have a Thanksgiving with her?" I asked.

"Indeed I would," he said.

As we came to my Hartford home, where I was to leave the train, I took his hand and urged him to do what would gladden his good mother's heart. He thanked me for my interest in his welfare. He promised to talk with his mother of our conversation. I urged him to commit himself to Christ as the all-sufficient Savior, and we parted.[3]

## Praising a Profane Sea Captain

Another illustration of the bait-principle of commendation, showing the importance of first winning a man to ourselves if we would later win him to Christ, and illustrating the skill by which honest commendation may be made effective, is found in a wartime experience of the chaplain.

Army-transport life gave many an opportunity of personal work with souls. Along the Atlantic Coast

the Civil War demanded frequent and varied use of
transports. At one time in North Carolina our
division made a raid into the interior of the state,
cutting itself off from its base of supplies, and
exposing itself to capture by a force of the enemy in
its rear. It seemed, both to us and to the enemy,
that we were hopelessly hemmed in; but, at the
close of the day in which we had accomplished the
main object of our raid, we turned directly toward a
river, and on reaching its banks found a number of
small vessels waiting there to receive us, in accordance with the plan of our commanding general.
These transports had been brought up to this point
so that we might board them, and quietly slip down
the stream during the night, thus flanking the force
that had come into our rear.

Boarding those vessels and getting under way
was an exciting movement. If the enemy discovered
our position in season to attack us before we were
fairly started, there was little hope of escape for us.
The skipper of the craft on which our regiment
embarked was a character. He felt the responsibilities of the hour, and he gave evidence of this in his
superabundant profanity accompanying every order
which he issued. I had never heard such abounding
and varied oaths as he poured out in the half hour
from the time we began to come on board till we
were fairly afloat and were moving down the stream.
Of course, then was no time to begin preaching to
him.

I could merely watch and study him. But that I
did, with real interest.

When, at last, all was quiet, and the evening had

come on, and the old skipper was evidently gratified with the success of the movement so far, I accosted him with complimentary words as to the skill and energy he had shown in his command.[4]

The bait was cast. But suppose, instead, that the chaplain had begun his conversation with an expression of regret at the skipper's profanity, and had called his attention to the bad example he was setting, and the harmful influence he must be exerting among the other men. How much further, and with what profit, do you think that conversation would have gone? That bait of commendation, on the other hand, was readily taken, as it always is.

This opened up a conversation, in the course of which he told of other exciting experiences he had had in other parts of the world. I listened attentively, and he saw that I was appreciative and sympathetic.

To be a good listener is one of the surest ways of winning and holding men. The "I can help you" attitude is fatal in this work; the "you are helping, or interesting, me" spirit is one of the secrets of success.

Presently he spoke of a particularly perilous time he once had on the coast of Africa.

"Ah, Captain! I suppose you had charge of a slaver then," I said.

Seeing that he had "given himself away," he replied, with a quiet chuckle:

"Yes, Chaplain, I've been up to purty nigh ev'rythin', in my time, 'cept piety."[5]

Is it not remarkable how sure the "opening" is to come when we are looking and praying and planning for it?

> "Well, Captain," I responded, "wouldn't it be worth your while to try your hand at that also before you die, so as to make the whole round?"
>
> "Well, I suppose that would be fair, Chaplain."
>
> The way was now open for a free and kindly talk. As we stood together there, on the vessel's deck, going down the stream by night, we talked pleasantly and earnestly, and I got at the early memories of his boyhood life in New England. Then I knew I was near his heart.[6]

There might not have seemed to be much in common, a few hours earlier, between the young Connecticut chaplain and the weather-beaten, profane sea captain. But that the younger man had already succeeded in winning the other to himself personally, as a powerful aid in winning him later to Christ, comes out in what happened that first night.

> By and by, all of us made ready for the night. There was but one berth in the cabin. That was the captain's. Our officers were to sleep on the cabin floor. The captain said to me:
>
> "Chaplain, you turn in in my stateroom. There's a good berth there."
>
> "No, no, thank you, Captain," I said. "Let the Colonel take that."
>
> "It isn't the Colonel's room; it's mine, and I want *you* to take it."
>
> "It would never do," I said, "for the Colonel to sleep on the floor while I slept in a berth. But I

thank you just as much for your kindness, Captain."

I lay down with the other officers on the cabin floor. While I was asleep I felt myself being rolled around, and I found that the captain had pulled his mattress out of his berth, and laid it on the floor, and he was now rolling me on to it. I appreciated the gruff kindness of the old slaver-skipper, and my heart was drawn the closer to this new parishioner of mine. Nor did I lose my hold on him when we were fairly at New Berne, at the close of this trip. I was again with him in the waters of South Carolina, and he came again and again to our regimental chapel-tent on St. Helena Island to attend religious services there. I saw that I had a hold on him.[7]

The most hopeful indication we can ever have in this work comes when one whom we would win shows an interest in the spiritual welfare of another. How the chaplain's heart must have been gladdened at this sign from his skipper-parishioner!

One weekday he called at my tent, having a brother skipper with him, whom he introduced to me, and then fell back, leaving us together. He joined my tentmate, the adjutant, and stood watching while I talked with the newcomer. He told the adjutant, with a string of oaths, that his foolish friend didn't believe there was a God, so he'd "brought him over here for the chaplain to tackle." It was fresh evidence that life was stirring in him, and that therefore he wanted another saved.[8]

Did it pay, to begin by seeking and finding something to commend, honestly and heartily, in a cursing old sea captain, and then to hold lovingly to him in the effort to show him his real Captain? See the end:

> When the war was over, I heard of that slaver-skipper in his New England seaport home. At more than sixty years of age he had come as a little child to be a disciple of Jesus; he had connected himself with the church, and was living a consistent Christian life. He was honestly trying his hand at "piety" before he died, and so was completing the round of life's occupation. For this I was glad.[9]

## Questions for Study and Discussion

1. What shall we think most about as we prepare to speak with someone on the subject of his relation to Christ?
2. What is "tact"?
3. What is the immediate purpose of our seeking to know the man and his interests?
4. Name two kinds of bait that are effective in man-fishing.
5. By what method, using which kind of bait, did Jesus win certain disciples to the work of His Kingdom?
6. Have you ever known anyone whose interests were all and wholly unworthy? Have you ever been surprised to discover worthy interests in one in whom you had supposed they were lacking? Describe the case.

7. When a person's chief interests are wholly removed from, or even antagonistic to, Christ's interests, how can you go about helping him?

8. Have you ever tried winning an indifferent or an unfriendly person by commendation? Describe the case.

9. What was the critical point in the conversation with the young whiskey drinker in the railroad train?

10. What is the chief objection to criticism or denunciation in this work?

11. What was apparently the single possibility of commendation in the whiskey drinker? In the profane sea captain?

12. What attitude is fatal in this work? What attitude is sure to draw people to us?

13. Why is it a duty for the soul-winner to strive to draw men to himself personally—to be liked, in other words?

# Seeking Common Interests

## Questions to Ask Yourself Before You Read the Chapter

1. If a worldly man whom you wanted to win should ask you what you meant by being "saved," what answer would you give?
2. What has Christ's salvation to do with this life and the affairs of this life?
3. Did Christ Himself emphasize chiefly men's future or present need of Him? Illustrate by Gospel passages.
4. Give your own definition of saving faith.
5. Should you say it is usually hard or easy to become interested in another's interests?
6. When you are seeking to win one whose creed or denominational tendencies may be quite different from your own, what is your best course?
7. Are any interests of another too trifling for us to utilize? How do we draw the line between worthy and unworthy interests of another? How far should we be willing to go in entering into another's activities in order to win him?

# 5
# Seeking Common Interests

**A** CHRISTIAN man was urging his friend to give himself to the Savior. "I know you do not believe you can save yourself," said the first. "Do you know of any Savior other than Jesus Christ?"

The man thus questioned faced his friend squarely, and said, "May I ask you a question? What do you mean by being saved?"

Then it was that the first speaker had to consider, more carefully, perhaps, than he had ever done before, what he *did* mean by being "saved." To show any vagueness or uncertainty in defining his belief would be disastrous to his influence with the one whom he longed to help. Yet he believed that it would be equally disastrous to use "stock phrases" with this man, who from his boyhood had been brought up in a Christian home of exceptional strictness, and who was, as he claimed, too familiar with conventional religious views and talk. Other circumstances added to the difficulty. The man was, far beyond the average, clean-living, morally high-toned, honorable, aspiring, interested in the best things. But he was not at all sure that there is any life beyond the present, nor did he find the average church or preaching of special interest to him.

The important thing for the soul-winner was to answer the honest question in terms of the present interests of the questioner. His first move was to pose a counter-question.

"Are you satisfied with yourself?" he asked.

"Not by a good deal," came the unhesitating reply.

"I knew you well enough to be sure of that," said the first man. "Have you always been able to accomplish what you want to accomplish in your life?"

"Far from it," was the answer.

"Let me tell you, then, what I mean by being saved," said the one who was urging the Good Tidings. "I have never found a man yet who was satisfied with himself. And I have never found anyone who satisfied me, except Jesus Christ. I discovered long ago that I could not live a single day satisfactorily in my own strength. Christ has enabled me to come nearer to my best than I have ever been able to do alone. By being 'saved,' I mean saved to one's best, enabled to make one's life count for the most. That is what the Savior has done for me."

A very inadequate and "temporal" definition of salvation, you say? Certainly, it was only a partial definition, but it was enough to set thinking in a new line a man who had previously supposed the Christian's idea of salvation to be chiefly the holding of a golden harp, and freedom from hell fire, through eternity.

A little later the friend who had presented the subject of salvation made clear to the other that he had no uncertain convictions as to the next world, and as to this life being only a beginning or preparation for the next. There was no argument or discussion on this point. But it would clearly have been unwise to urge the question of salvation in relation to the life beyond as the *first* thing for consideration by one who had, or claimed to have, doubts as to a life beyond. The man was willing to admit his need of help in this life. From that as a starting point it was well to begin.

## Making Salvation of Present Interest

There is a truth emphasized by this incident that ought to have a large place in the thoughts of every confessed follower of Christ. Are we not too much inclined to relegate salvation to the next world, as a kind of benefit payable upon death, the definite securing of which was finally accomplished when we stood up and confessed the Savior before men, and the principal value of which is for another world than this? Our Lord said nothing about men needing Him more after death than in present life. He did say, of Zacchaeus, "*This day* is salvation come to this house." And He added, "For the Son of man is come to seek and to save that which *was* lost"—not "which was to be lost."

To be "saved," then, means that present life here on the earth becomes a different thing. It means that the disappointing struggle to which the unsaved are doomed in this life, and to which the exceptionally moral man already referred to confessed as his own experience, shall give way to a life of achieving something that brings satisfaction instead of dissatisfaction. It does not mean that we are going to be satisfied with ourselves, or satisfied with our work. But it means that we have found a Person, a Savior, with whom we can be satisfied, and in whose service assured victory, as over against continued defeat, is found. It means that life takes on a fullness, a richness, an abundance, that is possible only through that Savior. If one who has not accepted this salvation asks, "How am I to know this? Why should I

believe it?" the answer comes from Christ's followers with
ringing, triumphant confidence, "We know it because we
have tried it. You may know it for yourself if you will." It is
not necessary to make the service of Christ seem an easy
thing, for it is not. But it is important to make the way of
salvation simple. Remember Bushnell's definition of faith:
"Faith is that act by which one person, a sinner, commits
himself to another Person, a Savior." Anyone can understand
that.

Not only at the moment of approach is it important to be
thinking of the other man's interests in order to begin with
them, but the principle holds throughout the work of soul-
winning. We must not only begin there; we may have to stay
there for a long time if we would exert any influence that is
really to count for Christ. This truth is unmistakably emphasized in the New Testament. Not only at the beginning of the
apostles' ministry were others drawn to them ". . . because
that every man heard them speak in his own language. . . .
speak in our tongues the wonderful works of God" (Acts 2:6,
11), but Paul evidently made this a permanent principle of his
evangelistic work:

> For though I be free from all men, yet have I
> made myself servant unto all, that I might gain the
> more. And unto the Jews I became as a Jew, that I
> might gain the Jews; to them that are under the
> law, as under the law, that I might gain them that
> are under the law; to them that are without law, as
> without law, (being not without law to God, but
> under the law to Christ,) that I might gain them
> that are without law; to the weak became I as weak,

that I might gain the weak: I am made all things to
all men, that I might by all means save some.

1 Corinthians 9:19–22

Were not these the tactics he had in mind as he wrote later
to the same converts:

And I will very gladly spend and be spent for
you; though the more abundantly I love you, the
less I be loved. But be it so, I did not burden you:
nevertheless, being crafty, I caught you with guile.

2 Corinthians 12:15, 16

There is the guile, the bait, the deep-laid planning that
Christ and Paul used and that we must learn how to use, most
gladly spending and being spent if we would hope to take
men alive. The work was costly to them; there will be little
virtue in our work unless we make it costly to ourselves. The
question is not, "Am I naturally interested in this person and
his interests?" but "Am I willing to *get* interested?" For we
always can if we will.

And it is always possible to disarm antagonism and win
confidence by this sinking of self-interests and deliberate
cultivating of another's interests. An instance of this occurred
in a boardinghouse experience:

One winter, some time after the Civil War, I
passed a number of weeks in a Southern city with a
young friend who was there for his health. All this
time we were at a well-filled boardinghouse. Most
of the persons there were those whom I then met
for the first time. A young gentleman who sat just

opposite me at the table, and with whom I naturally came to have a speaking acquaintance, was a person whose habits of life and ordinary occupations were obviously different from mine, so that our sympathy would not be promoted by conferring over these. Indeed, I learned, from the proprietor of the house, that when he understood that a New England army chaplain was coming to the house as a boarder he wanted to leave the house on that account, and was only prevented from doing so by the crowded state of that winter resort.

This certainly did not present an attractive opening for personal religious conversation. Yet I had learned that God gives us opportunities and responsibilities, in this line, which are of His choosing rather than of ours; so I waited for signs of God's leading. Meantime I endeavored to show to my tablemate that we had things in common that were to be recognized and enjoyed. To win his confidence to me was a duty, if I would hope to lead him toward Christ.[1]

When, after some weeks of this exchange, the time came for the chaplain to leave, he realized that he must now speak the direct personal word for which he had been trying to prepare the way. He reproached himself for not having done so earlier, yet even now he was in doubt as to whether he had won the man sufficiently to make his words of any avail.

I spoke of the matter to my roommate and companion, for whose health I was at the South. I suggested that perhaps it was my duty to go to the room of my fellow boarder that very afternoon, and say a word to him for Christ. He might, indeed, take offense at it, but, again, he might not. Was it not worth while taking such a risk for a soul's sake, and for Christ's? The decision was made. We kneeled together in our room, and asked God's blessing on my undertaking. Then I arose and started out. The room of my fellow boarder and his wife was but just across the hall from ours. Yet it was not an easy task to venture knocking at that room door, in the fulfillment of my purpose and my duty.

At my knock, the young gentleman whom I sought opened the door, and invited me in. His wife sat on a sofa. They welcomed me cordially, and when I told them that I purposed leaving the place the next morning early, they expressed regret, saying that our conversations of the past few weeks had been very pleasant. I replied that I had enjoyed knowing them, and that it was because of my growing personal interest in them that I had now called at their room. Then I explained that my joy in Christ's service was the greatest possession of my life, and that because I longed for my fellow boarders to have that joy, I had come to say so. The gentleman said that it was kind of me to say this, and that he had been thinking that he would like to know more about the religious belief I had, so that he might share it. Would I tell him what books he should read, in order to learn about this?

I replied that I could mention good books for him, but that I should much prefer to talk on the subject with him personally in detail.

"It would be very pleasant," he said, "to put

myself under your guidance, if you would instruct me."

"But I leave town early tomorrow morning," I said, "and I am cut off by this from helping you."

On his asking where I was going, and learning that I was to visit another part of the South, he responded that he would be glad to accompany me. On his asking his wife if that would be agreeable to her, she expressed her willingness to make the move, and it was arranged accordingly. Early the next morning that boarder who had wanted to leave that house when he found that a clergyman was coming there, with whom he could have no sympathy, finally left the house with that clergyman in order that he might be personally instructed in the religion which he had come to desire as his own possession. Surely God was leading. And God ever leads those who are willing to be led, even though they often follow reluctantly![2]

But—and one may say it in all reverence—God Himself could not have led to this result unless a child of His had been ready to pay the cost of studying and seeking another's temporal interests, in order that, by guile, he might be led to higher and better things.

## Ignoring Differences of Creed

There can be no barrier between any two men sufficient to prevent their finding common ground if only one of the two is determined that they shall. Least of all need differences of creed or faith keep men apart, though these are often allowed to do so.

When God brings us alongside of one whom we
may help, or may feel a responsibility for, we are
not to consider the obstacles, or difficulties, in the
way. God will take care of them. Nor are we to be
hindered by religious or denominational differences
that seem to stand between us and him. The one
question is, Can we evidence to him in such a way
as to impress on him the surpassing love of God and
the blessed fullness of the spirit of Christ? We are
not to risk the repelling of him by making prominent the things wherein we differ; but we are to
approach him at the one "point of contact," that
from a connection at that point the electric current
of sympathy may quiver to the extremities of his
being.

In my experience I have had occasion to meet and
converse with individuals of various religions, or
nonreligions, and I have never found our differences
a real barrier. "Every heart is human," and God's
love is suited to the need of every human heart. Our
duty is to follow God's lead, nothing doubting.

One winter Sunday morning, in a country place
in eastern Massachusetts, I found myself a guest in
the home of the superintendent of a Sunday school,
at the anniversary of which I was to speak in the
afternoon. In the forenoon of that day I was to
address a congregation several miles from my
present stopping place. My host was to transport
me over, in his carriage, for my morning appointment. Accordingly I found myself, that very cold
day, tucked in, under a heavy robe, in close
quarters, in the buggy, with the Irish driver. It was
evident that that man was just then the "every

creature" in the world for me to teach the Gospel to, and I had no right to expect a blessing on my labors for the rest of the day if I failed in my duty to him while on my way to my next appointment.

To begin with, I told my seatmate whither and why I was going. This was to indicate my confidence in him. Then I said, as showing my interest in him and his standpoint:

"You are a Catholic, I suppose?"

"Yes, sir," was his reply, with a tone that seemed to indicate a conscious barrier between us.

I at once spoke of several Roman Catholic bishops and priests with whom I was well acquainted, and whom I valued, and then asked:

"Have you a Catholic church in the village?"—which we had just left.

"There is no church there yet, sir. But a priest comes over once in four weeks, and says mass."

"When is the next time for his coming?" I asked.

"He's there today, sir."

"Then I'm keeping you away from mass. How sorry I am for this!"

"Oh! it's all right, sir. I'm glad to go with you, sir."

We were on the same plane at this time. It was now my duty to improve this advantage. And I began:

"You say you're a Catholic; are you a good Catholic? Do you honestly love God, and trust your blessed Savior, as you are taught, by your church, is your duty?"

"I'm afraid I'm not a good Catholic, sir. I'm afraid I do not do my duty."

What better start could you ask for an earnest talk to anyone? At this starting point I pressed home the truth:

"My friend, when we think of what the blessed Jesus did for us, how He left His glorious home in heaven, and became a babe in a manger to begin with, and then toiled on here and suffered for years, and was despised and rejected of men, and was crucified and died, in proof of His love for us, and of His Father's love, in order that we can be saved, is it asking or expecting too much of us that we should show our gratitude in the little things that Christ asks of us?"

"No, sir, it is not."

And of this sacred theme we talked together pleasantly, on that carriage seat, that Sunday morning, until we reached our destination. My new host, a clergyman, welcomed me to his home, while he directed the driver, with his horse, to the stable. On entering the parsonage, I said to the pastor that, as the day was very cold, I should be glad to have the driver invited into the kitchen out of the cold. Accordingly, he went to the barn to invite the man in. Returning, the pastor told me that the man said he wished to go to church to hear the gentleman preach that he had just brought over.

As I rose in the pulpit, I saw my seatmate of the morning facing me in a pew. What he had heard from me about his Savior, and about his duty to that Savior, had apparently sharpened his appetite for more. I confess that some of the words of my address that morning were for that one hearer, rather than for the body of the congregation. Then, as at many times before and since, one person was more to me than many persons. As, at noon, we drove back together, our conversation was again on the theme of themes, with fresh comments on phases of it about which I had talked, in his hearing, from the pulpit.

On thinking the day's work over at its close, I realized, not that a Protestant and a Roman Catholic had found much that they could talk about together to their mutual spiritual profit, but that we two, who had met together as seatmates on that cold Sunday morning's ride, might have been profited by the talk even had we been two Presbyterian elders in conference in revival time.[3]

## Going Where the Other Man Is

The secret of getting successfully interested in another is simply that we deliberately put ourselves mentally into that one's place. It takes mental effort and sacrifice of easygoing comfort to do this, but not exceptional genius. The old story of the lost horse is a familiar one. The whole village had turned out to find the horse, but had failed. Finally a youth who had the reputation of being somewhat feebleminded led the horse home. Upon being plied with questions as to how he had done what everyone else had failed to do, he quietly explained. He had first ascertained where the horse had last been seen. "Then I went there," he said, "and I just said to myself, 'now where would I go if I was a horse?' And I went there, and there he was." It was not only a simple method, but the only one. We have got to learn to go where the other fellow is if we want to find him.

An incident in a well-known pastor's experience illustrates this with telling effectiveness:

> "Yes, I want to come into the church; have been wanting to come for fifteen years," a woman said to the minister when he urged her to confess Christ at the next communion. "But I'm waiting for Jim. You know he's a good man, yet he doesn't have much use for the church, or—begging your pardon—for preachers. He tells me to go ahead, and stop waiting for him. Many a time I've made up my mind to do just that. Then, at the last minute, I think if I wait just a little while longer, surely he'll come with me. What would you do?"

The minister told her the best thing she could do would be to become a church member without further delay, for she would have a better chance to influence her husband as a professed Christian than as an outsider. Before the call was concluded, she agreed that this was her best course.

As the minister left, he said, "Please remember me to Mr. B. when he comes home; tell him I am sorry to have missed him, and that I hope to have a good talk with him soon."

A few days later he met Mrs. B. once more. "Jim made me promise to tell you something for him," she said, much embarrassed. "He says if you want to see him so much you will just have to go where he is."

"And where is that?" was the inquiry.

"Hadn't you better wait a few days before going to him? Then he'll be where the likes of you can get

to him better. You see, today he's working on the
last section of the steeple of the new church."

It was enough. The minister made up his mind
he would find Jim that very afternoon. At the
church—a magnificent building with a lofty spire—
he learned that his quarry was indeed at the top.
"You can't get to him, though; nothing but ladders
to climb on; better let us call him down," the
foreman suggested.

But the minister had been challenged to go
where Jim was. So he climbed ladder after ladder
until—nearly two hundred feet above the street—
he found a much-surprised man. A few minutes
were spent in very satisfactory conversation. Then
the minister climbed down to make other calls.

The next Sunday, Jim became a member of the
church his wife had already joined, and was there-
after known as an earnest Christian man. His
friends wondered a little at the change in his life;
but the only explanation he would give was this:

"The preacher who'll climb two hundred feet of
ladders to call on me can have me every time!"[4]

A young man of pronounced agnosticism but of scholarly
scientific interests once came into Dr. Trumbull's horizon.
There was no common ground at all, in spiritual matters, to
begin with. The older man, however, learned—by making it
his business to learn—that the younger student was deeply
interested in a certain line of scientific study. Promptly he set
out to know something of that subject himself. He spent some
weeks in reading up on it. He gathered books on it, every one
he could lay his hands on. Then one day he mentioned to the
young student that he had several books in that field at his

office, and he invited him to avail himself of them whenever he cared to look them over. The subject became a theme of mutual interest, and the younger man eagerly seized opportunities of discussing it with one who knew so much more about it than most persons he met. From that common ground, reached only by the costly sacrifice of time and study by the soul-winner, it was not difficult to lead on to spiritual matters; and the day came when the once-agnostic thanked God and his confessed Savior that one man had been willing to be "all things" to him.

This seeking of the "other fellow's" interests was a secret of the success of the founder of the Young Men's Christian Association, Sir George Williams. His biographer tells a characteristic incident of his young manhood:

> George Williams was possessed also of that extraordinarily rare virtue in a young man—tact. He was wont to say, when asked as to the means he suggested for tackling a young man, "Don't argue, take him to supper," and in more than one instance he carried out his suggestion literally. In reviewing these early days, George Williams used to tell the story of how they won over to their side one of the young fellows in the house who was most active in his opposition, and whose conduct was a terrible ordeal for their faith. He held a good position in the business, and, as George Williams relates, "we could not get near him in any way. When any young fellow gave his heart to Christ, he would pounce upon him and say, 'We'll soon take all that nonsense out of you!' "
>
> This young man was the organizer and chairman of the "free-and-easy" held on Saturday evening at

the adjoining tavern, "The Goose and Gridiron," and largely frequented by Hitchcock & Rogers's assistants. In a short time he had promoted a very active and vigorous campaign against these young men of the upper room, and naturally he was at once marked out by them for special and particular prayer. For many weeks they waited in vain for sign of change. His hostility increased in vehemence and bitterness.

The best part of one evening's meeting was devoted to a discussion as to the most likely means of getting into touch with this most unsympathetic young man.

"Can anyone tell me," said George Williams, "if there is anything he is especially fond of which we could give him? Can we do anything that will overcome his dislike for us?" One of those present suggested with a touch of humor that he had a passion for oysters.

"Let's give him an oyster supper, then," said George Williams. "Who is the best man to invite him?"

They selected one who was on comparatively friendly terms with the chairman of the "free-and-easy," and in due course he was casually informed that a number of the young fellows were going to join in a big oyster supper, and would be glad if he would accompany them. The idea of these Christian young men indulging in such frivolity amused him immensely, and in a spirit of bravado he accepted their invitation.

It was a lively evening for all concerned, and all enjoyed it, for George Williams had given strict instructions that no attempt at persuasion was to be made on that occasion. Their avowed enemy, finding himself in such pleasant company, came to the conclusion that these young men were not so bad as he had thought. As a return for their hospitality, he consented later to attend one of their meetings. The sequel is best told in an extract from the diary of George Williams's friend, Edgar Valentine, who writes in May 1844:

> In the course of the day George Williams came to me and said he believed something particular was going to happen today, inasmuch as the Spirit's operation seemed visible in our midst. A young man by the name of Rogers was seriously impressed about his soul's salvation.
> The next morning Rogers was still more concerned, and William Creese, noticing his attitude, said to George Williams, "George, what is up with Rogers?" "I do not know," he replied, "but I feel I cannot pray for him any longer. I was praying for him this morning until it seemed as if I heard a voice from heaven saying to me 'Yes,' and I knew he would be converted." Shortly afterwards Rogers definitely threw in his lot with the little band of the upper room. His name is to be found among the first twelve members of the Association.[5]

The question sometimes arises as to whether a soul-winner may properly interest himself in any and every interest of another man's in order to influence and win him. The answer to that question is plain and unmistakable. One may devote himself to any interest under the sun that is not actually wrong or harmful in its effects. It is never necessary to depart one jot or one tittle from Christ's standards in order to win men's confidence. But it is often necessary to depart a long way from our own natural interests in order to meet another on common ground. We must never let down; we must often go far afield.

Another question that is sometimes asked is whether one may not make the mistake of spending too much time over the temporal interests of a single individual in the hope of leading him eventually to Christ. Should a pastor, for example, spend a solid half day, or day, or even more, in getting work for a man out of a job, in order to prove to that man his genuine interest in his bodily welfare, when that pastor might in the same time speak a word for Christ to perhaps a score of other souls?

Can there be any real doubt as to which method has Christ's approval? We are not in this work chiefly for numerical results. Christ did not work that way. Once men get the impression that a pastor or a neighbor cares only for their souls and not at all for their bodies, his influence over them is gone. As Wilfred T. Grenfell, the English physician who spent his life reclaiming the bodies and souls of the Labrador fisherfolk, has said: "Is not the real problem of Christianity how best to commend it to the world? Can we afford to divorce the 'secular' from the 'religious,' any more than the 'religious' from the 'secular'? It seems to me there is only one way to reach the soul—that is, through the body. For when the soul has cast off the body we cannot reach it at all."

## Questions for Study and Discussion

1. Give a definition of salvation that should appeal to a man who claims to be in doubt about the next world.
2. What mistake of emphasis should we avoid in talking and thinking of spiritual matters?
3. Give Bushnell's definition of faith.
4. How long may we need to study another man's interests in winning him to Christ?
5. Quote Paul's statement as to the importance of seeking others' interests in seeking to save them.
6. What is necessary to the removing of a barrier which is preventing two men from finding common ground?
7. When talking with one whose creed differs from our own, is it well to emphasize the differences of belief, or to emphasize points of agreement? Why?
8. What common ground can always be found between Protestants and Catholics?
9. What common ground should you say can always be found between Jews and Christians?
10. What is there in our going where the other man is that is likely to attract him to us?
11. What suggestive advice of six words was Sir George Williams fond of giving to soul-winners?
12. How far may we go in identifying ourselves with another's interests?
13. What did Grenfell say as to our duty of giving prominent attention to men's bodies and secular interests?

# The Place of the Bible in This Work

## Questions to Ask Yourself Before You Read the Chapter

1. What is your own thought as to the use of Scripture quotations in individual soul-winning?
2. Is there any danger of a tendency to use the Bible as a fetish? Give illustrations of such use. How should that danger be guarded against?
3. Wherein is the Bible like other books?
4. Wherein is the Bible different from all other books?
5. Under what circumstances should you say a Bible quotation would be most effective?
6. Under what circumstances should you say a Bible quotation would be least effective?
7. Now formulate a principle for the use of the Bible in individual soul-winning.

# 6
# The Place of the Bible in This Work

THE Bible is the soul-winner's indispensable equipment. But it is not necessarily his tool. A moment's consideration of the principles already studied will show why. Ninety-nine persons in a hundred, of those who have not yet come to Christ, are not deeply interested in the Bible. A Bible text is not, as yet, attractive bait to them. The fact that the Bible *ought* to be attractive to them has nothing to do with the matter. We are working with men as they are, not with men as they ought to be. If they were already just where they ought to be in their interests, they would be in no need of our attention.

Recognizing, therefore, that the Bible and its teachings have little place in the chief interests of the great number of those whom we would reach: If we would use bait that shall attract them at the outset, and seek interests that are common to them and ourselves, we must, as a rule, begin with something other than a Bible quotation.

This principle was one of Christ's principles in the work of individual soul-winning, and is in accordance with all that we know of human nature, and of God's approved ways of dealing with men. It underlies successful man-winning in every sphere of life. Don't expect the man whom you would win to begin with your interests; begin with his.

Apply the test to some of the actual instances of successful soul-winning that we have already studied. Take the case of the whiskey-drinking seatmate in the railroad train. What would have been the outcome if, after the flask had been proffered, the soul-winner had begun his conversation with the impressive words, "Wine is a mocker, strong drink is raging." Probably some such answer as, "Then I guess I'll do my raging back in the smoker, stranger," and that day's opportunity would have come to an abrupt ending with the man's exit.

Or suppose the young army chaplain, hitherto unknown to the profane old skipper in charge of the perilous transport expedition, had introduced himself that evening with any of these phrases: "Swear not at all." "Let your speech be Yea, yea; Nay, nay." "Thou shalt not take the name of the Lord thy God in vain." Just what likelihood is there that the skipper would have been so won to the stranger as to have offered him his cabin for that night?

The point is not that those Scripture passages do not contain truth which those two men sorely needed to consider. But the men were in no state of mind to listen to Scripture passages at the outset. Later on, when that old skipper had "come as a little child to be a disciple of Jesus," he probably treasured some of those very Scripture passages as safeguards of his life. But this was because he had been talked to first of all in his "own language," which was not the language of the Bible, and about his own interests, which were not yet Scriptural or spiritual.

## H. Clay Trumbull's Habit

Dr. Trumbull was a devoted Bible student from the time of his conversion till the day of his death. So absorbing a place did Bible study fill in his life that he believed he might be permitted to continue his Bible studies in the next world. His regular daily plan of Bible reading was to read the Book through from Genesis to Revelation, short sections at a time, turning back to Genesis to begin again after he had finished. In this way he read and studied and reread and restudied every word of the Scriptures through a long lifetime. He drew his strength and knowledge, his convictions, his hopes, his guidance, and his life, from the pages of that book. I have the little pocket Bible, in its tattered buckskin case, which the army chaplain kept close to him as more of a protection than his sword and his pistol during the dark days of the Civil War.

Yet an examination of the experiences in individual soul-winning that are the basis of our present study shows that Dr. Trumbull rarely *quoted* Scripture when he was first seeking to win another to Christ. The reasons for this we have already seen.

Once when he was asked about how he used the Bible in his soul-winning, he wrote:

I fear I may startle you, if not indeed shock you by frank answers. I was never a theological student, nor a pastor. My training has been wholly practical, among men as they are. I have been an army chaplain and a Sunday school worker. Hence, my ways are unconventional; and not like those you are taught in the books.

I have not been in the habit of using Bible texts or Bible language in my talks with individuals. I talk in the most natural and direct way with my fellows about their duty and their desires. If I used a Bible text, some conventional or erroneous meaning may have been attached to it by the person to whom I am speaking. I seek help, and, in a sense inspiration, from the God of the Bible; but I want everything fresh from Him for the case in hand.

## When the Bible Is Common Meeting Ground

Of course, if we find, as we may in an exceptional case, one who is not Christ's confessed follower yet who is greatly interested in the Bible, then the Bible may be the very meeting ground of common interest that we can properly seek. Such an unusual case as this is illustrated in the experience of George F. Pentecost:

A few questions developed the fact that he was a cultivated young German, the son of a German rationalistic theologian. He had been but a short time in America. He told me that he was fond of study, and especially philosophical study; and gave good evidence of familiarity with the various schools of thought, current and past. He said he had been led to think of Christianity as an ingenious mythology (having a very slender thread of historical truth in it), more or less the product of an early enthusiasm that had exalted Jesus into Deity.

He was frank and candid, saying that he was free to admit that a careful reading of the New Testament revealed a purer and altogether better system of ethics than that of any of the philosophies with which he was acquainted; and that the whole book had an air of sincerity and truth about it. But there were several insuperable difficulties in the way of his acceptance of it as truth.

I asked him to state his difficulties, which he did in about these words:

"There are three chief claims set forth in the New Testament, upon the truth of which, it seems to me, the whole system must stand or fall."

"What are they?"

"Why, first of all, it is claimed all through the New Testament that Jesus was the Son of God; *i. e.*, God manifested in human nature—a supernatural Being. This He claimed for Himself, and even died in defense of the claim; for, if I am not mistaken, that was the charge upon which He was put to death by the Jews; viz., that in claiming to be the Son of God He made Himself to be equal with God—which was, under the Jewish law, blasphemy. Certainly He seems to have believed Himself to be God; and so also did His apostles, especially John and Paul."

"Well, what is your next difficulty?"

"Why, the next difficulty is that our salvation depends, not upon the uprightness of our own lives, but upon the fact of Christ's death, which is represented as a sacrificial act—what Mr. Moody calls 'the atonement.' "

"Well, what is the other difficulty?"

"The resurrection of Christ from the dead. Everything in Christianity depends upon that."

"Well," said I, "now why are these things difficulties to you?"

"Why, I cannot possibly believe that Jesus was God. He could not be. And it is not possible for anyone who was *really* dead to rise again. Such a thing never was in the world, and it could not be. And even if it were so, I do not see how anyone

could be saved on account of another's death, and
not on account of his own uprightness."

I confess that the task before me seemed very
great indeed. But he seemed guileless in his desire
to know the truth; and so, with a prayer in my heart
for help, I said:

"Well now, let us look at the first difficulty—the
incarnation. As I understand it, you are a Theist.
You believe in the existence of a personal, eternal,
and omnipotent God, who is the Author of the
universe and of our being?"

"Oh, yes!"

"Very well. Now, with that for a starting point,
you cannot philosophically hold that the incarnation
is an *impossibility—that it could not be.*"

A very little talk ended in his admitting the
*possibility* of the incarnation, but denying the
*probability* of it. And then he went on to say, with
the quickness of thought and the clearest per-
ception of the whole matter:

"But I think Jesus was Himself deceived. I grant
that He may have, in moments of enthusiasm,
thought He was the Son of God; and that He did at
times make this claim there is no doubt. But at
other times He certainly made such statements as
forbid us, on His own testimony, to believe that He
was equal with God; indeed, He admits that He is
an inferior being. In fact, Christ's own testimony
concerning Himself is contradictory.

"And this leads me to question the truth of the
Gospels; and so to reject Christ as the Son of God,
and hence Christianity itself. For Christianity is
nothing but a beautiful delusion, if Christ is not

what He claims to be. Now He says in one place, 'I and my Father are one' (John 10:30); and again, 'He that hath seen me hath seen the Father' (John 14:9); and, as I have before said, when on trial before the high priest He still claimed, and that in the face of certain death, that He was the Son of God (Mark 14:62; Matthew 26:64). But He said on another occasion that His Father was greater than He (John 14:28). Now He cannot be one with God, and at the same time inferior to God. And He says, 'All power is given unto me' (Matthew 28:18). Now that is an admission that He had not power *Himself*, but it was given to Him; and surely He that *receives* power is inferior to Him that *gives* it. Now are not these contradictions in His own testimony? And do not they destroy the worth of it entirely? It seems to me that, whatever of truth there may be in the historical existence of Jesus Christ, He only *imagined* that He was the Son of God; and that in speaking of Himself, He spoke according to the *mood* He was in, sometimes believing Himself to be the Son of God."

After hearing him through, I turned to the passages he had referred to, and having read them aloud, I said:

"Let us suppose that you had been on earth when Jesus was here, and had heard Him make these contradictory (?) statements; and had asked Him, saying, 'Master, I do not quite understand you. A little while ago you said, "I and my Father are one," and, "He that hath seen me hath seen the Father"; and again you say, "My Father is greater than I," and, "All power is *given* me." How can you be one

with the Father, and yet less than the Father? And
how can you be equal with the Father, if your
power is given to you, and is not yours independently?' And suppose He had said in reply, 'My
child, what if, *for the purpose of your redemption* from
sin and the curse of the law, I *voluntarily laid aside my
eternal glory,* and suffered myself to be born of a
woman, and made under the law, thus *limiting my
being* to the *conditions of your nature,* that I might, in
that nature, offer up to God such a sacrifice for sin as
would enable Him to proclaim forgiveness of sins to
the whole world? In such a case can you not conceive
that there is no contradiction in these sayings of
mine? For indeed, *I am* one with the Father, and he
that hath seen me hath seen the Father; but for
purposes of atonement I have *voluntarily assumed an
inferior position,* that I might thus take your place and
die, which I could not have done unless I had taken
a subordinate place, yea, and your very nature. Thus
I sometimes speak of my *eternal relation to God,* and
sometimes of my relation to Him as the *messenger of
the covenant* sent forth to redeem.' "

He listened attentively to this; and then said, as
if speaking to himself:

"Yes, that might be; I can see how that might be.
But" (speaking to me) "did Christ ever make such
an explanation? Is that the theory of Christ's subordination to the Father?"

In answer to this inquiry I turned to the second
chapter of Philippians, and said:

"Certainly this is the explanation of it; for see,
Paul was trying to inculcate lessons of humility, by
exhorting the Philippians to voluntarily take a sub-

ordinate place in relation to each other, though they might, as a matter of fact and right, stand on an equality; and enforced his exhortation by this reference, 'Let this mind be in you, which was also in Christ Jesus: who, being in the form of God, thought it not robbery to be equal with God' [thought not His equality with God something to be contended for]: 'but *made himself* of no reputation, and took upon him the form of a servant, and was made in the likeness of men: and being found in fashion as a man, *he humbled himself*, and became obedient unto death, even the death of the cross' " (Philippians 2:5–8).

He took my Bible in his hand, and read the passage over and over himself, and said: "Wonderful! Wonderful!" And still holding the book in his hand, with quivering chin and moistened eyes, he said:

*"Yes, the Son of God made Himself of no reputation* FOR ME; *and took my nature, and died on the cross* FOR ME!"

And then, looking up into my face, he said:

"What have I got to do about it?"

To which I replied:

"Accept Him; believe on Him; and confess Him as your Savior."

"May I?"

I replied, opening my Bible to Romans 10:9: "If thou shalt confess with thy mouth the Lord Jesus, and shalt believe in thine heart that God hath raised him from the dead, thou shalt be saved."

"Let me see that!"

I handed him the book, and he read it aloud, and then said:

"I do believe in my heart that God raised Him

from the dead; and I do acknowledge Him as my Savior."

We dropped down together upon our knees (with a little group which had gathered about us); and I offered a brief prayer of thanksgiving to God for his conversion, and a little petition for his keeping.

Thus was the young Rationalist converted.

It will be seen at a glance that no attempt was made to meet his objections by an exhaustive argument, but by simply presenting the biblical statement to him, leaving the work of conviction to the Holy Spirit. As a mere argument, the statement may have been very defective; but God can take His own truth and use it more mightily than the strongest argument man can construct.

The man who was won had come of his own accord, because of his interest in Christianity, to a place where he hoped to get light. He was interested in the Bible at secondhand, and needed only wise guidance to the truths of the Bible at firsthand. He had specific difficulties of interpretation of Christianity; when those difficulties were met by one whose familiarity with the whole Bible enabled him to meet them, the man's course was clear. Without such Bible knowledge, Dr. Pentecost would have been helpless. Here the Bible as the worker's equipment became also the worker's tool.

## The Principle Restated

To restate, then: We must *know* the Bible by persistent, exhaustive, lifelong study. We can never make its precious, lifesaving truths too thoroughly a part of our minds and hearts and being. It is the Guide Book to the Way of Life, not only for ourselves, but for those whom we would win. And our work with them is not complete until we have brought them to a recognition of the Bible which shall give it the same unique place in their lives that it has in ours.

But this leading of men to the Bible is to be accomplished, as a rule, by wisely recognizing that those whom we would win to Christ are probably not interested in the Bible to begin with: that their attitude is more likely to be indifferent or even antagonistic to it at the start. This being so, we shall do better to make our approach in the language of their everyday life and in the terms of their present interests, leading them later, with loving skill, to the Book without which any life is sadly incomplete.

### Questions for Study and Discussion

1. What is, and what is not, the relation of the Bible to the soul-winner?
2. Why is a Bible quotation seldom the best bait to begin with in seeking to win a soul to Christ?
3. In accordance with what principle must we determine when to use Bible verses?
4. What was Dr. Trumbull's method of personal Bible study?
5. What was his practice as to quoting Scripture in individual work?

6. What reasons did he give for not using Bible texts?
7. When does the Bible furnish a good meeting ground of common interest?
8. What were the three difficulties of the young German unbeliever?
9. Describe just how they were met by Dr. Pentecost.
10. State the exceptional features of the young German's case. Show how they made his case different from most cases of everyday opportunity in individual soul-winning.
11. Restate the principle that determines the place of the Bible in individual work.

# Conviction Better Than Discussion or Argument

## Questions to Ask Yourself Before You Read the Chapter

1. What is discussion? What is argument? What is conviction?
2. Name some "borderline" questions of conduct concerning which even Christian people disagree.
3. Under what circumstances is it proper for one man to tell another man his duty?
4. What objections can you think of to giving discussion and argument a place in individual work?
5. What is the best way to help a man to decide all borderline questions correctly?
6. What characteristic, among the men that you know, seems to give a man the greatest influence with other men? How do you account for this?

# 7
# Conviction Better Than Discussion or Argument

THERE is only One in the universe who can safely tell a man his duty as to the details of everyday life and practice. Therefore it our chief duty to lead our fellows to that One, and to seek to win them to a loyal acceptance of Him as their Head and Guide and Savior, so that He may settle their questions of duty for them. It is never our duty to attempt to settle for our fellows such questions as God intends they shall refer to Him. About the only duty that one man can safely and unconditionally prescribe for another man is the supreme duty of surrender to God's will.

Unwillingness or failure to recognize this simple truth has caused many an earnest worker to become a stumbling block rather than a guidepost to those whom he honestly longs to help. Many a promising spiritual conversation has gone to pieces on the rock of discussion of details of personal duty. Let us avoid this error as a snare and a pitfall. The devil will have little to fear from our efforts at individual work if we let them become debates over borderline problems in everyday life.

An actual incident from Dr. Trumbull's experience (which

we discussed somewhat in chapter 5) will make the practical application of this truth plainer.

My companion was different from anyone with whom I had ever conversed personally on the theme of themes. He had not been, while a child, under the religious training and influences with which I was most familiar. Hence there seemed to be no such common basis for a preliminary understanding as I had been accustomed to find. Yet this necessitated a coming down to first principles, which, after all, had its decided advantages in such a conference as this.

"My friend, would you like to be saved?" I asked at the start.

"Indeed I would," he replied.

"Do you think that you can save yourself?"

"I certainly do not," was his response.

"Do you know of any Savior to be trusted except One?"

"I do not," he said heartily.

"Well, now," I said, "there is no necessity of your reading any books on the subject, to learn the way of salvation. [He had asked what books he might read in order to learn more of the subject.] Let me see, here and now, if you are willing to be saved by the one Savior in His own way. Understand that I do not make any conditions or requirements of conduct or practice, in order for you to be saved; but I will ask you this question, in order to ascertain your attitude toward the whole subject. Suppose you were to find that Jesus Christ wanted you to refrain from [I mentioned several questionable activities] would you give them all up, or would you feel that there were some of these things that you could not refrain from?"

My friend thought the matter over with evident seriousness, and then he gave this intelligent answer:

"Well, Mr. Trumbull, I might have different views from yourself about some of those activities; but if I were convinced that Jesus Christ wanted me to refrain from any one of those things, or from them all, I should be willing to conform my conduct to His wish."

"That's all that I want to know," I said. "I lay down no requirements. I want Him who is to be your Savior to be your guide. Now just go to your room and kneel down before the Lord, and tell Him how it is. Tell Him that you need a Savior, that you do not know any Savior other than Himself, and that you want Him to save you. Tell Him that you are willing to put yourself into His hands, that you will conform your conduct and course to His wishes, and that you want to trust Him."[1]

To ask a man to let Christ settle his problems of duty for him is better than to try to settle them for him ourselves. The latter never does any good, and often does great harm. The outcome of the sensible and only safe procedure in this instance was significant. The man became

an earnest, devoted follower of Christ, as I was familiar with him for precious years and in different spheres. He became a close student of the Bible. He and his wife together made an open confession of their new faith, and connected themselves with a prominent church in New York City. They became active in mission-school work, and he devoted his trained business mind to perfecting methods and systems of work, so that he was known widely throughout the country as a leader and guide in that field. He became, after a while, prominent as one of the most influential workers, and director of other workers, in the entire country.

In his personal habits and conduct he became strict and careful, in the line of our talk that evening.[2]

Notice what Horace Bushnell, the famous molder of theological thought of the middle of the last century, had to say of the principle of refraining resolutely from discussing or dictating another man's personal duty:

When I, later, told Dr. Bushnell, to whom I had introduced the young gentleman, of that conversation, and of the outcome of it, the good Doctor said, characteristically:

"That shows how much easier it is to do a big thing than a little thing. If you had begun to discuss with this man, at that time, any single habit or practice, you might never have got beyond it. You would have been stranded on the first barrier. But to ask him to trust the whole thing to his Savior, and be guided by Him, was the better way. If one is right at the center, he is likely to get right at the circumference."[3]

As with discussion over details of duty, so with argument over points of belief. Neither discussion nor argument is likely to draw men closer together; both tend rather to keep men apart. As such, both are to be resolutely avoided in a work which seeks above all else to win others to us, not to keep them at a distance.

But there is a power that we may and must have in this work, and which utterly outdistances any seeming but empty skill in discussion or power in argument. It is the power of conviction. That power is nearly irresistible. It will win if anything can. It will swing a man over from false belief to true unless he is bound to the false forever.

A man's *belief* of what he proclaims goes far to make it believed by others. So long as he himself has any doubt on the subject, he is not likely to convince those who are in doubt. This is true in every sphere of life. If a man sees his neighbor's house on fire, in the dead of night, his wild, ringing shriek of "Fire! Fire! Fire! Get out! Get out! Your house is on fire!" sounds out on the midnight air with a force that is itself convincing. All who hear it know that the one who utters it feels its truth, and wants others to feel it.

How different it would be if a man should knock timidly at the house door, and say gently that he had reason to think that a fire was kindling in the vicinity, and that he thought it would be well to look into the matter! How could he expect dull sleepers to be aroused on such a call? If his knowledge did not stir him more than this, how could he expect those yet asleep to be aroused from their torpor by him?

Peculiarly is this the case with one who sounds a call to stir a sluggish soul to action, in view of truth that he deems precious and all-important, but which the other is not very anxious about or fully convinced of. Any show of doubt, or indecision, on the part of God's herald, is calculated to shake the confidence of the hearer of the message. This has been found to be the case by every gospel preacher, or winner of single souls, in any sphere. Every show of earnestness, or evidence of intense conviction, on the part of those who stand for Christ, gives added weight to each word of the message from the Captain of our Salvation. Hearty Governor Andrew, of Massachusetts, said of Abraham Lincoln, when he had assumed the presidency, "I'm glad we've got a man who believes something." If a man would have another believe something, he must believe something himself.

Intense conviction, showing itself in intense personality, marks the difference between an ordinary leader, or counselor, and an exceptional one. It was not the number of his soldiers, but his power to use every man as if he were ten men, or a hundred, that made Napoleon, or Phil Sheridan, the general that he was. Surely he who has Christ back of him in his every word and his every deed, ought to feel that he is wielding the power of the Almighty when he acts or speaks for his Savior in that Savior's work.[4]

Let our conviction, then, of the truth and joy of our message, shut out argument or discussion forever from our methods in the art of taking men alive. And our conviction may be twofold: the conviction that we know our message is true, and the conviction that the other man knows it is true. This latter, building on the image of God that is in every man, is one of the most disarming attacks we can make against the opposition of unbelief.

## Resolute Refusal to Argue

As illustrating the positive effectiveness of conviction, along with a firm refusal to be drawn into a discussion, note the following:

> An earnest young clergyman in New England, whom I know well, began his ministry in a parish where his predecessor had lacked strong conviction, and had encouraged, if not cultivated, doubts. The new clergyman's beliefs were startling to his congregation. One Sunday, after the service, a bright young man came up to the minister, and said:
>
> "I don't believe what you are preaching, and I want to discuss your beliefs with you."
>
> "Well, my friend, there's no use in our doing that. I am convinced, and you don't want to be. I am sent here to preach the truth that I believe, whether my hearers believe it or not."
>
> Weeks went on. The minister saw his young friend, Sunday after Sunday, in the gallery. One Sunday the minister invited all who wanted to converse with him on the matter of personal religion to come to his study on Monday evening. That evening this young man appeared. Coming up to the pastor's study table, where the pastor sat, he said:

"I am here tonight, not for argument, but for counsel. I've watched you and have heard you for weeks. I know that you have got something that I haven't. Now I want you to tell me how I can get your crucified Christ."

The preacher was ready to help that seeker. And another soul was won to Christ through the counsel of a believer who had convictions.[5]

Another worker, whose strength lay not in skillful words but in his simple conviction as to Christ's love and what that love had done for him, had occasion to put this matter to the test.

He was accustomed to ride out from Boston daily to and from a suburban town. One who was frequently his seatmate was a man prominent as an unbeliever, and who edited a free-thinking periodical. Again and again this man endeavored to draw my friend into discussion on the subject of religion, but without succeeding in so doing. One day my friend openly met the matter in this way:

"I do not want to have a discussion with you on the subject of religion. I'm no match for you in argument. You'd get the better of me every time. But, apart from that, one thing I know, that the Lord Jesus Christ is my Savior, and I trust Him all the time. This is the comfort of my life, and I wish you had the same comfort."

At this his pertinacious seatmate brought his hand down sharply on his friend's knee and said heartily:

"There you've got me, my friend. I've nothing to offer against that."

My friend's conviction was his best and his resistless argument. "I know whom I have believed" will convince another if anything will. No method of discussion will take its place with any hearer.[6]

And still another instance shows that while a pugnacious unbeliever may be surprised, even startled, by the blunt, insistent phrasing of an honest disciple's conviction, he is more likely to be won by quiet tenacity here than by intricate argument.

I was in an office where I occasionally had business, and, as I was talking with the proprietor, I said, as he asked my opinion in a matter of principle:

"The Bible says so and so."

"*What* Bible?" he inquired sharply, almost defiantly.

"The Bible," I replied to this question, quietly but firmly.

"Muhammadans have one Bible. Buddhists have another Bible. Jews have another Bible. Chinese have another Bible. Which Bible do you mean?" he responded.

"*The* Bible," was my response.

"Well, I suppose I know what you mean."

That was a point gained to start with. He admitted that "*The* Bible" was not to be put on a plane with the others, so that he was really in no doubt on the subject.

"But," he added, "I don't agree with you as to
the value of the Bible."

"I'm sorry," I replied.

"You think, I suppose," he went on to say, "that
the Bible is God's Word."

"Of course I do."

"Well, won't you try to prove to me that it is so?"

"No, indeed."

"Wouldn't you like to have me believe the
Bible?"

"Of course I should."

"Well, then, why not try to convince me?"[7]

Just here came the answer that startled this polemic
would-be disputant out of the ruts of his ordinary and
self-satisfied lines of thought. He had asked the "why" of the
other's refusal to attempt "logical proof," and he got it:

*"If God has failed in this, with all that He has done
for you in a third of a century, I don't propose to set my
little hazelnut brain at the task at this late day."*

"Why, then, won't you prove to me that God is
what you believe Him to be?"[8]

To this question there came another answer that must have
sunk in deep, not for its arguing power, but by the sheer
weight of the immovable conviction that lay back of it:

"The subject is too sacred for ordinary discussion. I wouldn't consent to discuss with you the
question whether my mother was really my mother;
yet God is dearer to me than is my mother or my
father."

At this I left the office without further comment.[9]

That even the unbelieving disputant was ready to recognize the believer's position as a fair one appeared from what followed.

A few weeks later I was there again. He said:

"I understand, Mr. Trumbull, how you feel about the Bible; so I won't ask you to discuss it. But have you any objection to telling me what you understand the Bible to teach on certain points?"

"Not in the slightest," I replied.

Then the way was open for a frank, free, and reverent conference over the teachings of the Bible; and the man who had been a scoffer was ready to be told the truth as to Bible teachings by one who had no doubts on the subject, and who therefore commanded confidence. Several such conferences as this seemed to bring this man into a different attitude toward the Bible and its teachings. After a longer absence than usual from Boston, when I was once more in the office of this man, he said to me:

"Mr. Trumbull, will you tell me just where is your home?"

As I told him, he said:

"I've been very sick. I thought I was going to die, and I wanted to send for you."

Then, as if to show that he had not wholly abandoned his disbelief, he added:

"Not that I was really troubled about myself or my beliefs, but you seem so confident in your beliefs, that, if I was going to die, I wanted you to talk with me."[10]

He was yielding hard; but he was yielding. And it would seem probable that he never would have made even the reluctant admission that he did to one who had met him on his own lower ground of debate concerning precious truths that are above and beyond debate. The opportunity was wider open now than ever before

> for a free talk about Christ and his salvation, which I tried to improve for that needy soul. "For their rock is not as our Rock, even our enemies themselves being judges." We surely ought to be confident in our beliefs, and impress others by this confidence, as we seek to win them to their Savior and ours. We have every advantage, and we should show this in our loving labor for souls.[11]

Even in that most difficult of all efforts, the winning back to Christ of one who has abandoned his discipleship, it is conviction that has the power which argument would utterly lack. The chaplain had cause to remember this from a wartime encounter.

> When first I joined my regiment in North Carolina, I found there a young lieutenant, whom I had known as an active, earnest Christian worker in his Connecticut home. As I was looking up the members of my new charge, I called on him in his tent, and said something of my hope to have his help in work for my Master.
> "No, no, Chaplain," said he, "I've given up all that stuff. I know now that there's no truth in it, and I don't want to hear a word on the subject."[12]

How tempted most of us would have been to "argue that point" with the young backslider! How much better than argument was this statement of the chaplain's earnest conviction, coming with somewhat of the startling unexpectedness of a blow between the eyes:

> *"You are not saying now what you believe, Lieutenant."*

The braggadocio was all gone as the young fellow asked, in genuine surprise, of a man who had dared to meet his statement of intended conviction with a counterstatement whose conviction seemed to ring even truer:

"What do you mean, Chaplain?"

And the earnest, kindly answer came back:

"I mean that I know you well enough to understand that what you said and did, for years, in your faithful Christian work and in your Sunday school teaching, has not been given up by you out of your inmost heart. You can talk this way to me now, to try to stiffen up your courage of resistance; but when the camp is quiet, and you are alone on your bunk in the darkness, you would never talk in this way to your God, who you know is near you always."

"Well," he said, somewhat more gently, "I don't want to talk about this subject, at any rate."

"But I must talk about it," I said. "It's very real to me. And I'm here because of my belief. I love you too dearly to refrain from speaking to you, and

urging you to come back to your old love and faith
and duty and joy."

Weeks passed on. When I saw the Lieutenant in
his tent I would show him that I, at least, hadn't
lost my faith; yet I refrained from provoking any
discussion on the subject. He seemed to be grateful
for my interest in him, and he never again gave an
expression of his unbelief, nor did he say that which
would jar on me. I tried to reach him by indirect
means, in talking about former interests and persons connected with our work together for our
common Master. In this way, at times, the truth we
had both then held dear would come into prominence; but no word of unpleasant difference was a
result.[13]

It is discussion and argument that bring on unpleasant
differences, never straightforward, honest conviction. What
was the end of this effort in which the believer would admit
of no doubt?

After a little there came on a battle in which our
regiment lost severely. Several temporary hospitals
were opened in small dwelling-houses in different
parts of the field of action. As I was occupied in one
of these hospitals, I heard that my lieutenant friend
lay wounded in another. As soon as I had opportunity, I went over to see him. His right leg had been
amputated near the hip. He lay on a cot among
many wounded. Looking up as I approached he
said cheerily:

"The Lord has got me, Chaplain. I wouldn't
serve Him with two legs, so He took away one. But

now I'll be more of a man with one leg than I was
with two."

Then as I spoke warmly of my sympathy with
and interest in him, he told of his experience and
feelings.

"As my leg went out from under me, and I felt I
was gone, I said, 'The Lord's got me, and I'm glad
of it.' You were right, Chaplain, that day you came
to my tent first, I never really gave up my belief, or
had any rest in my life trying to live without faith.
And now I believe I shall live nearer the Lord than
ever, and have more comfort in Him."[14]

It was like that old-time wrestling match at the ford of the
Jabbok, when the Lord touched the thigh of a man who had
been persistently fighting Him, and the rebel was crippled,
and the crippling brought a changed life and a new name.
Crippled into new life!

The convictions of the chaplain-friend were bearing fruit:

He was confident that he should soon be restored
to health, and that he should use his new strength
in the Lord's service. I had pleasant interviews with
him as he talked of his plans in Christ's service, and
he gave convincing evidence of his Christian love
and faith. But the shock of the amputation was
severer than he at first supposed, and he soon sank
away to his final rest. The prodigal had returned to
his loving Father's home.[15]

## Questions for Study and Discussion

1. What duties can one man safely and unconditionally prescribe for another?
2. What error should we earnestly guard against in doing individual work?
3. What is the best way to help a man to settle his problems of personal life and conduct?
4. What did Bushnell say about center and circumference?
5. What effect are discussion and argument likely to have upon men's relationship to each other?
6. Give your own explanation of why intensity of conviction is such a power in working with men.
7. What two convictions may we have in this work?
8. What is the Christian's best answer to skilled and intricate argument against his belief?
9. When, should you say, is it well to give such blunt answers to men as that of the minister ("I am convinced, and you don't want to be"); or that of Dr. Trumbull ("If God has failed in this," etc.)?
10. Why does our conviction of belief have special effectiveness in working with backsliders?

# Encouragements
# and Incentives

## Questions to Ask Yourself Before You Read the Chapter

1. Name the encouragements that you have had from your personal experience in individual soul-winning.
2. Name all the encouragements that you can think of from the experiences and principles so far studied in this volume.
3. What would you say is the greatest incentive we have to the doing of this work?
4. What instances of rebuff by those approached on the subject of personal religion have you known in your own or others' experiences?
5. What prospect of success would you say there is in approaching one who knows beforehand that we intend to seek to win him?
6. Is it a duty, or not, to work with those who are mentally deficient? Describe any instances you have known.
7. Under what circumstances should we expect and urge an immediate decision for Christ?
8. When is our full duty to an individual discharged by a single conversation with that one?

# 8
# Encouragements and Incentives

IF it is true there is an abundance of special and peculiar difficulties in the work of individual soul-winning, equally true is it that there is a richness of unexpected encouragement and uplift in the work. Every one who has obeyed the Master's call to make disciples of others can testify to this with a glad heart. Indeed, the encouragement is so constant, and the rewards are so rich, that the wonder is that the devil succeeds as well as he does in keeping us fainthearted!

One of the most frequent experiences that lifts one up is the unexpected disclosure that God has been preparing the way for us: that those whom we thought indifferent or reluctant are eagerly awaiting a word. This was illustrated by a boardinghouse experience of Dr. Trumbull:

> For a long time my family and I lived at a boardinghouse in a New England city. One noonday I suggested to my wife that we ought to speak to our table neighbors personally and urge them to surrender themselves to Christ. I proposed that while I would go up to the gentleman's place of business and have a talk with him, she should seek

out the wife in her room, and plead with her for Christ. This was agreed to. Then we knelt together and asked God's blessing on our efforts, and on those in whose spiritual welfare we were interested.

The gentleman was a bank officer. I called there just after bank hours. As I asked him for an interview, he invited me into the directors' room, and closed the door. When I spoke of my loving interest in him, and of my purpose in calling, he burst into tears, and said that he was so glad I had come. Then he told me how he had longed, day after day, for someone to speak to him on this subject. How adroit some Christians are in avoiding the subject of personal religion in business places and in business hours! I found this man longing to be helped into the Kingdom, and glad to learn the way.

When I went back to the house, at the close of the afternoon, my wife told me of her experience. After my leaving her, as she was preparing to go to the room of the wife she had on her heart, there was a knock at her door. As she opened the door that wife came in, and, bursting into tears, she asked if her friend wouldn't help her to Christ. She had longed to be spoken to by someone, and now she could bear this no longer. The two wives went on their knees together, and they rose with glad and grateful hearts.

That husband and wife soon stood up and confessed their faith together, as they connected themselves with the church.[1]

Two surprises in one day! Two needy souls, eager and longing for Christ if only someone in Christ would show the way!

Even when we are sure that there is little hope of winning a certain person because of that one's known attitude of opposition, we are likely to be encouragingly disappointed if only we will make the trial. Take the difficult case of one who knew beforehand that certain people would endeavor to win him to Christ, and who had no sympathy with the idea.

At one time I passed a Sunday in the home of a superintendent of a village Sunday school in Connecticut. It was a humble home, back in the country, and no member of the family seemed to have had any special educational advantages. Yet not only the spiritual atmosphere of that home, but its religious exercises and methods, were such as to command my respect, and to make me wish to commend them to others. This led me to ask how all this came about, and, in consequence, I learned this instructive story.

The church of which this man was a member was an ordinary Connecticut church, not given to new things, but keeping on, year after year, in its tried and approved course. But in some way it had been led to try the experiment of having every family in the congregation, or parish, visited by appropriate members of the church for religious conversation. Possibly it was in connection with the labors of an evangelist, but of that I am not sure. My host, who was now the superintendent, was then not a member of the church, nor was any one of his family. He had heard of this proposed movement, and as he sat in his home one day he saw one of the deacons and another church member drive up to the house and

get out for a call. So far from having any special
interest in this, he spoke jokingly of it.

But when the deacon was in the home of that
man and his wife, speaking with them for Christ as
he had never spoken before, they felt the power of
his words, and when he knelt with them in prayer
they were ready to commit themselves to the Savior
in a sense of need and trust. Their Christian life
was started at that time by that individual word to
them, as all the sermons and pulpit appeals for
years before had not influenced or been felt by
them. From that hour that was a Christian household, every child feeling its influence for good. And
soon that newcomer into the Kingdom at middle
life was chosen superintendent of the Sunday
school because he was a better man for it than any
man who had been trained from childhood in the
church.[2]

Suppose the soul-winning deacon had passed by that family
because of the "hopelessness" of trying there! He never
would have gained the encouragement that must have been
his all through the years as he watched the results to that
household and to the church and to the whole community
from that single appeal for Christ.

## Rebuffs Almost Unknown

It is a noteworthy fact that it is a rare, almost an unknown,
experience for one to meet a rebuff when courteously and
earnestly expressing an interest in another's eternal welfare.
Yet this is not strange. Everyone recognizes that the man who
seeks to win another to Christ has no "axe to grind," no

ulterior motive. There is encouragement here for us all, timid and reluctant as we are. Of his traveling experiences Dr. Trumbull wrote:

> I have had hundreds of such conversations with seatmates on the car, seatmates whom I had never seen before, and whom I never met again. I never had such a conversation which I had reason to regret, or which seemed to be distasteful to my companion. And many such a conversation has brought out the warmest side of a fellow Christian.[3]

Similar testimony could be had from every individual worker. The biographer of Sir George Williams, founder of the Young Men's Christian Association, writes of him:

> When he crossed the Atlantic he made a point of speaking to every soul on board from the captain to the stoker, from the poker-players in the smoking-room to the emigrants in the steerage. And the remarkable thing is that, although he must have spoken thus of their souls' salvation to tens of thousands, he could never recall a single instance when he received a rude or mocking retort, a splendid tribute to the way in which the world is quick to recognize and appreciate, and pay homage to, true Christian sincerity when accompanied, as it was in the case of George Williams, with the rarest tact and most modest courtesy.[4]

## What of the Mentally Deficient?

Is there any gain in working with those who are mentally substandard, slow of intellect, or actually half-witted? Are we not doomed to discouragement if we attempt it? Can they

appreciate what it is to do right, or to come to Christ? Will not
the Lord care for them anyway? Two army experiences gave
Dr. Trumbull a conviction as to this field of effort that he
never relinquished.

The army brought all sorts of persons together,
and I had to become acquainted with and interested
in them all. While at St. Augustine, Florida, in the
winter of 1863–64, a part of our regiment did
garrison duty at the old Spanish coquina fort, with
its bloody memories and its weird legends of former
occupants. I was accustomed to hold Sunday school
services each Sunday afternoon, and also midweek
evening services, in the little chapel opposite the
main entrance of the fort. Just outside of that
chapel there was a pile of rusty cannon, on which
men would sometimes loll while we were having
services inside. And as I moved about the fort I had
many a talk with men whom I rarely met so
familiarly elsewhere.

One day, in walking through the fort, my attention was drawn to a strange face glaring through an
iron-barred opening of a dungeon door in the
southwestern corner of the casemated walls. It was
the most repulsive face I had ever seen. Low-
browed, coarse-featured, dark-complexioned, with
small black eyes under shaggy eyebrows, and thick
sensuous lips, it seemed like a cross between a
Digger Indian and a New Zealand native. The
expression was one of low cunning, with a mixture
of hate and derision. It was an unhuman face, yet
the man who bore it was evidently one of my
parishioners, or he would not be where he was.

"Who are you, my friend?" I said. "Where do you belong?"

He answered in a low, gruff voice, as if he were resenting an attack.

"I belong to the Tenth Connecticut."

"You belong to the Tenth Connecticut!" I said. "Why, then I'm your chaplain, and I've got an interest in you."

As I kindly questioned the man, I found that he had been most of the time since his enlistment in confinement for insubordination, and therefore I had not met him. After a brief talk I left him. Soon he was released from confinement, and was again with his comrades. I saw him occasionally, and spoke to him kindly, but I did not look upon him as a hopeful case in comparison with others, and had comparatively little to say to him.

After a while, we left Florida for Virginia. As we moved up along the coast in a crowded transport, this man came to me in the throng, and said softly:

"Misser Chaplin, I want to talk to you."

"Well, I'm always glad to talk to you," I said. "But where can we go to talk? Let us lean over the steamer's rail. That is our only place to talk by ourselves."

As we leaned there together, he told me his strange, pathetic story.

"Misser Chaplin, you 'member when you talked to me at the dungeon door. You spoke kind to me. You said you's my chaplin. I never forget that, Misser Chaplin. I'm a rough feller; I never knowed much."

Then with a chuckle and a leer, as he thought of

his Ishmaelitish life, he said: "I *did* worry my cap'n. And he hated me. Ten months with ball and chain! A hard time of it! But what you said at the dungeon door's all true. And what you said in prayer meetin' is all true."

"Prayer meeting!" I said. "I never saw you in prayer meeting."

"No, I was jus' outside, on those old cannon. And now, Misser Chaplin, I want to do right. Misser Chaplin, I suppose we's goin' into a fight, and I want to do my duty. They say I'm a coward. I've never been in a fight, but I want to do my duty."

Then in a voice strangely tender in contrast with the first gruff utterance which I heard from him in the dungeon, he said: "Misser Chaplin, you're the only man who ever spoke kind to me. If I get killed I want you to have my money. And if I get killed, won't you have it writ in the paper that Lino died for his country?"

We reached Virginia. We were in a fight. Lino bore himself so bravely that his captain, whom he had worried so long, called him out before the entire company, at the close of the engagement, and commended him for his bravery and good service. Hearing of this, I looked him up after the fight was over, and congratulated him on his well-doing in active battle.

"You've done bravely, I hear, Lino, and I'm glad of it."

"Yes," he said, with a softer chuckle than before. "They called me a coward, but I tried to do my duty. 'Tain't always the frisky ox that's at the far end of the yoke."

That long-friendless man showed, in his way, his intention of doing what God would have him do. Who of us has better improved his opportunities?[5]

An even more striking encouragement, in the way of result, came from a tardy recognition of the rights of those who lack other advantages to a saving knowledge of Jesus Christ.

Among the recruits picked up in Connecticut, for the sake of the bounty, in the later years of the Civil War, were some men who would not have been accepted in the army on their merit. One such man in our regiment was below the physical standard, and he seemed beneath a fair average of intelligence. He was a laughingstock in the regiment. He was not competent for a soldier's duty. He was unable to drill. So he was put at a menial duty, and became a byword and a butt. I do not think that it occurred to me, at that time, that he was a proper subject for religious conversation. I am speaking of what was, not of what ought to have been. Possibly the confession of my lack will suggest to someone else the impropriety of such a failure.

One day, in St. Augustine, as I was walking on the parapet of the old Spanish fort, I came upon this man. No one else was just then in sight, and it seemed as if it would be taking nothing from others if I said a word to him. So I stopped to talk with him. Calling him by his regimental nickname, I asked:

"Do you ever pray?"

"I say 'Our Farther,' " was his thick and drawling response.

"Who is your Father?" I asked.

That question he couldn't answer. He had only, by someone, been taught by rote to say the words of that prayer. Then I took him as a little child, as, indeed, he was a little child in intellect; and I told him of God as his loving Father in heaven, who would be glad to have him pray to Him. And I told of Jesus and His love. He listened like a glad child who was taking in a child's lesson, and he seemed to comprehend what I was saying, as well as any of us can comprehend these truths. From that time I had a new interest in that soldier boy, and he seemed to be showing signs of awakened life. He welcomed my interest in him, and he responded gratefully to every word of counsel or suggestion from me. I reproached myself that I had not been readier to estimate him as God estimates every soul whom the Savior loves and died for.[6]

The immediate response of this needy and neglected child of God to the story of the Father's love had been a surprise and an encouragement to the chaplain. But who but the Father Himself could have foreseen the end?

After the war was over I was, one Sunday evening, to make an address in a Connecticut city. As I entered the outer door of the prominent church, a bright-faced young man stepped forward to greet me, calling me by name. As I looked the second time, I saw that it was that anything but hopeful soldier whom I first talked with on the parapet of the old Spanish fort in St. Augustine. On inquiry, I found that he had made a public confession of his faith in one of the prominent churches in that city, and that he was witnessing a good confession. He was a regular attendant in the Sunday school. As I looked at him, I hoped that I had been of some service to him; for I was sure he had taught me a good lesson—a lesson that I want to pass on to others. Any soul that Jesus loves is worth our best work in its behalf.[7]

Still another remarkable instance of this kind of work is found in the following experience of a missionary, President Browne of Harpoot College in Turkey:

One evening I was riding into one of our lowest villages in eastern Turkey, and my horse almost stepped upon something in the mire. As I looked, I saw a little humpbacked girl. When she opened her mouth, her utterance was more foul than the mud and mire beneath her. Arriving at the teacher's house, I spoke to him about that little humpbacked girl, and he said: "Don't tell me anything about that girl; she is a lost soul." I worked five days there in that village to persuade the parents of this little girl to allow her to come to our school. Within a year her heart had melted, a character had begun to develop, and her face became bright and hopeful. As the years went by, she developed a marvelous capacity for patience and love, and when from the villages came especially hard cases, we would bring them to her.

When she graduated, she was made the principal teacher in our college. She had rare talents for teaching; we had never seen anything like it before. But one day she came to me and said: "I am not contented to be a teacher in the college." "Why not?" I asked. "Why are you not satisfied here?" "I want to go," she replied, "to the places where others do not wish to go." So I sent her out to a place on the northern branch of the Euphrates, where she did a work that none of our teachers had been able to do. She introduced the Gospel and founded four churches. Think of it! This "lost soul" had founded four churches, in spite of her deformity and the early influences of her life.

## Is Any Opportunity Too Slight?

There is no such thing as a "trifling" opportunity in the work of soul-winning; no opportunity so slight that it may safely be passed by as not worth improving. A teacher of a Bible class saw, late one weekday afternoon in winter, a member of the class hurrying by his house. The man was going home from his work, that of a housepainter. The teacher waved a greeting to him through the window, but the man failed to see it. Thereupon something prompted the teacher to hurry out of the house, bareheaded, after his friend. He caught him at the corner, and they stood together chatting. Upon the teacher's asking the painter how he had been, he replied that he had had a pretty bad spell of sickness a few nights before. "I tell you," he said, "it makes a man think pretty hard when it seems as though everything was dropping away from him."

"But you're all ready to go whenever you *are* called, Joe?" asked his teacher with a hearty smile.

"I don't know about that," was the sober answer. "Sometimes I think I am, and then again I don't know." This came as a genuine surprise to the teacher, who had supposed that the man was in no doubt as to his relation to Christ.

It took but a few minutes' earnest talk there on the street corner to show this troubled soul that he need not be in doubt another moment. A meeting with the pastor was suggested, and gladly agreed to; and at the next communion service of the church the painter stood up and gave public expression to his acceptance of the Savior who would have all men ready for His coming. Would he have been thus ready if that teacher had felt that his duty was fully discharged in class on Sundays, or that the casual passing of his house was too slight an opportunity for a show of interest?

A personal experience impressed a Christian businessman with the measureless gain of counting no opportunity too slight.

He was on his way to an international convention of Young Men's Christian Associations in Montreal. As the train approached that city, a bright young man came into the car as a representative of a prominent hotel in Montreal, seeking guests for his hostelry. My friend inquired as to the location and advantages of the house, in view of the heat of summer, then prevailing. At once the young man waxed eloquent over the subject, and fairly convinced his hearer that this was the place for him.

As my informant arranged for a room there, he asked pleasantly of the zealous advocate:

"My young friend, are you a follower of Jesus?"

"I can't say I am, sir," was the reply.

"Well, if you were in Christ's service, and would plead as earnestly for His cause as you do for the hotel you now represent, you would be a valuable helper to your Master, and you might do a great deal of good to others. I wish you were in Christ's service, using your powers for Him."

The young man passed on through the car, and my friend went his way to the city, having simply said this word for his Master, as was his wont. It did not seem to be an exceptionally hopeful occasion, but who can tell?

Several years passed. My friend sat, one day, in his private office in a New England city. As he called out a question to someone in the hallway, his pleasant voice sounded through the building. Almost immediately a strange young man appeared at the office door, and said:

"Excuse me, sir; but, may I ask, did you not attend a convention in Montreal, about the first of July, a few summers ago?"

"Yes, I did, as I well remember; but what of that?"

"Do you remember speaking to a young man on the cars, and telling him you wished he would work for Jesus as faithfully as he was then working for a hotel in Montreal?"

"I think I do, now that you recall it."

"Well, *I* cannot forget it. Your words rang in my ears. They resulted in bringing me into the service of Jesus, and now I am trying to speak words for Him wherever I go. Being in this city on business today, I came into this building [where were the rooms of the Young Men's Christian Association], and as I was near your door I heard that voice which has been sounding in my memory all these years, and I have come to thank you for what you have done for me."

That delegate to the international convention of Young Men's Christian Associations did more by his word to an individual for Christ than if he had made half a dozen eloquent addresses in the convention.[8]

Bishop C. C. McCabe told of an illustration out of his experience that impressed him with the worth of the opportunity which most of us would consider no opportunity at all:

At one time in a strange city, as the driver got down from his box and opened the door to let me out, I paid him, and grasping his hand said, "Good night, I hope to meet you again in glory." I then went into the house, met my host, and retired. About midnight my host knocked at my door and said: "Chaplain, that driver has come back, and says he has got to see you tonight." When the broad-shouldered, rough-looking man, with whip in hand, was shown up, the tears rolling down his cheeks like rain, he said, "If I meet you in glory, I have got to turn round. I have come to ask you to pray with me."

How mistaken we are when we attempt to measure opportunity by man-made rules!

As John B. Gough said of the one loving word of Joel Stratton that won him: "My friend, it may be a small matter for you to speak the one word for Christ that wins a needy soul—a *small matter to you*, but it is *everything to him*." It is forgetting this truth that causes personal work to be neglected.[9]

How often—or how seldom!—do we speak to those who serve us in public places, such as waiters, streetcar and railway-train conductors, and sleeping-car porters? A prominent Sunday school leader, W. C. Pearce of Chicago, told the writer of a pleasant surprise he once had. Here is the incident in his own words:

I took the train at the Lake Shore Depot, Chicago, for a town in northern Indiana. I was very tired, and, although it was during the day, I took a seat in the sleeper, and almost before we had left Chicago I was asleep. I had instructed the porter to waken me before I reached my destination; accordingly, as we neared the end of the journey, he came in and aroused me. A few minutes later he returned to brush my clothes and help me with my baggage.

As he was brushing me off I remarked: "My journey ends before yours today, doesn't it?"

"Yes, sir," was the answer.

"I wonder which of us will come to the end of the journey of life first?"

"I don't know, sir, I don't like to think about that, sir."

"Well," said I, "it doesn't matter much if one has a through ticket."

The man looked puzzled, and said, "I don't know what you mean, sir."

Then I explained to him that I had secured a ticket at Chicago, which was nothing more or less than a promise of a ride, properly signed by the railroad officials. And I pulled from my pocket a small copy of the Bible, and spoke of Christ's free offer of salvation, quoting some one of the promises, and explained that this promise was signed and sealed by the death of Jesus Christ, and that I had accepted that promise and was trusting fully in the journey's ending right.

With a very happy face, which I shall never forget, he responded, "Bless the Lord, I have that." And he added, *"I have been a porter for many years, but you are the first gentleman that ever spoke to me about Jesus Christ."*

It is only by persistent practice in seizing every opportunity that we shall gain the keenness that can see an opportunity where most people would see none. We need not be afraid of seeing too many. For we miss so many! Think of the attitude among Christian people generally that would make such an occurrence as the following possible among intended ministers of the Gospel!

An active worker for individuals was visiting a well-known divinity school in order to have an interview with a student. While waiting for that student he was improving his time, as usual, by seeking individual souls near him. Encountering a janitor, or other helper, in the hall, he had a pleasant, direct talk with him. He found a soul

waiting to be helped. He led that soul to the Savior.
In conversation he found that although that soul
had been long in the vicinity of embryo preachers,
not a word had been spoken to him by one of them.
They were waiting to be eloquent to a full congregation. Why should they waste their strength on a
single soul?[10]

Those closest to us may be most in need of the personal
word for Christ. Only as we carry the commission ever-present
in our thoughts, to be obeyed as we go about our daily
business, in school or college, in the home circle itself, in
boardinghouse or hotel, on train and boat, have we any
assurance against missing priceless opportunities for soul-
saving. Our morning prayer should anticipate it as the biggest
thing in the day ahead. Our evening prayer should review the
day in relation to this. ". . . Lovest thou me? . . . Feed my
sheep" (John 21:17).

## Individual Work Always Needed

For nothing else will ever take the place of individual work
in bringing souls into the Kingdom. Without it, some are sure
to be missed. Faithfulness in pulpit or Sunday school class or
prayer meeting are good accompaniments of it, but never
substitutes for it. After the Civil War was over, the chaplain
had occasion to realize this, in his continued efforts both as
preacher and individual worker.

A regimental "pioneer corps" did peculiar army
service, and its members often exhibited high
qualities of courage and daring. They would go
before our column to cut a way through forest or

bushes, or to construct a bridge or road, sometimes under the enemy's sharp fire. To fill their place and do their work was to win honor and regard from officers and men. They would quickly construct a shelter for an officer, which gave him protection and comfort as he stopped for a night or a week. In doing this they showed rare skill and taste and made themselves indispensable to the command as a whole.

Some months after the war, I was announced to speak, one Sunday evening, in a prominent church in western Massachusetts. As I rose in the pulpit I saw in the congregation a well-remembered sergeant in our "pioneer corps." He was one of the bravest of the brave, always prompt and ready in whatever he had to do. Hearing that I was to speak, he had come to listen to his old chaplain. The pastor in whose pulpit I stood told me afterwards that this veteran soldier had a good name in the community, although he was not a church member. At once I felt that I must reach him for Christ. The chaplain must be faithful that night to the pioneer corps sergeant.

At the close of the service the brave old "pioneer" came forward to give me greeting. After a talk about our campaigning together, I asked him if he wouldn't go with me for a talk to the parsonage, where I was to pass the night. This he was glad to do. By the pastor's consent, I had a room where we could be by ourselves. In a free talk with my old comrade, I found him ready and glad to commit himself wholly to Christ. He only needed to know what to do, and to be helped to do it. When I asked

him if he was ready and willing to take this step
now, he assured me that he was. At this we went on
our knees together, and the brave soldier of country
became a trustful soldier of Christ. As I knew of
him afterwards, I felt that he was one of many who
needed only the being enlisted to be ready for
active, persistent service.[11]

Yet if the chaplain had let his work cease with his pulpit
address that night, the enlistment might never have been
made.

The best of prayer meetings, no matter how well conducted
and spiritual, will never accomplish the work of individually
seeking the individual. A young Christian army officer once
taught needed lessons in this line.

In each city to which he was assigned he went to
the Young Men's Christian Association as a hopeful
center and starting point. There he usually found
the weekly prayer meeting as perhaps the highest
point of spiritual devotion.

Going into such a prayer meeting, early in the
evening, at one time, he asked the leaders how
many persons had been sought out from the high-
ways and byways that evening. On being told that
nothing of the sort had been done, he asked that all
should kneel at once in prayer, and then all should
scatter to the street corners and drinking places and
gambling houses, seeking souls and urging them to
come in where they could be helped. Fifteen
minutes or more later they were to return to the
Association rooms, and then they might have a
hopeful prayer meeting there. The first experiment

was an eminent success, and its every repetition seemed an improvement on this. More of those for whom they had there hoped and prayed were gathered in in a single evening, under this plan of work, than under the old plan, or the no plan, in any one year before.[12]

And a young man who had been won to Christ by the simple word of individual appeal from a stranger wrote in an agony of earnestness:

"O Mr. Trumbull! you cannot urge the followers of Jesus in too strong terms to talk more of Him. A kind word may save a soul! That soul may save a thousand! Do they realize it? When I remember, at times, how my soul has longed, when a mere boy, a stranger in a great city, for someone to take an interest in me and my soul's welfare, I feel as though I should fly away for fear there is someone near me smothering the same awful feelings, and longing for that kind word of Christian sympathy.

"I remember very well, the morning I packed my things to go and fill that situation in that city, how my mother prayed for me, and said, as she thought of the temptations I should be subject to, 'O William, how I wish you were a Christian!' I wished so too. She hoped all would be right. When, that day, I went into the garden to say good-bye to father, as he saw me coming he turned his head to hide the tears, and he reached out his calloused hand, calloused for me, and said: 'You are going away from home, William, and all you have in this world is your good name. Keep that. Attend church

every Sabbath regularly somewhere, and you will
come out all right.' I promised him I would. I went
away very sad, but determined to keep my promise.

"For one whole year, Sabbath after Sabbath, I
attended one church and sat in the same seat, and
no one ever intimated that he thought I had a soul;
and I was never sufficiently acquainted with a
member of the church or congregation to be on
speaking terms; yet, at times, my sense of guilt was
overwhelming, and oh for a friend!" . . .

How many souls there are waiting and longing to
be blessed, as that Vermont boy waited and longed
in his first year away from home! One day, on
Broadway, I noticed a crowd about a little child.
Pushing in among others, I saw that it was a strayed
child. He was lost, and he knew no way of finding
himself or his dear ones. Seeing my look of tender
sympathetic interest in him, the child looked up,
and stretched out his hand to me, saying, in
pleading tones, "Won't you please to show me my
way home?" That cry has been sounding in my ears
ever since, when I find myself near a wandering
soul like that Vermont boy in the city, and like
others who are about us on every side, as we ride
and as we walk. There is work enough to do for
Christ if only we will help the individuals near us
who need our help, and who are ready to be
helped.[13]

## Pressing for an Immediate Decision

As to seeing definite results of our efforts in individual
soul-winning, that may or may not be our privilege. Our chief
concern must be the giving of the invitation to come to Christ.

The results are between Christ and the individual. Sometimes, perhaps often, we shall not know what the outcome is. Again, it may be our duty to press for immediate results, for instant decision. An illustration of this occurred in one of Dr. Trumbull's railroad train experiences.

One morning, as I was riding on a train in western Connecticut, I saw a young man whom I had seen at a religious meeting the evening before. I had never seen him except at that time; but there was a deep religious interest just then in the church where I had seen him, and accordingly I took a seat by his side and began conversation on the subject. He seemed glad to be spoken to about it, and I said I hoped he would enter into Christ's service with the others there who were doing so. He said he wished it were so.

"Then why isn't it so?" I asked. "You have nothing to do but to commit yourself at once to the loving Savior as His servant and follower. He is more ready to accept you than you are to offer yourself."

"Do you mean, Mr. Trumbull, that here on this car seat, just now, I can give myself to the Savior, and He will accept me without any further preparation on my part?"

"I mean just that," I said. "The Savior is ready when you are. There is no gain in your waiting; and no further preparation is needed than for you to be ready to give yourself to Him and to trust Him unhesitatingly."

He said not a word more about himself, but he

gave evidence of a loving, trustful soul, when he
reached out in thought after another, saying:

"Mr. Trumbull, I've a brother who ought to be a
follower of Christ. I wish you could talk to him."

That is one of the first evidences of the Christian
spirit and life, an interest in another soul, and the
forgetting of self in that care for another.[14]

Another occasion when the securing of an immediate
decision for Christ was a plain duty of the individual worker
occurred in an army interview:

One evening, as I was returning to my evening
quarters, I saw the gleam of a faint light through a
low shelter tent in our regimental camp. It was long
after "Lights Out" had been sounded, and I
stooped and scratched at the tent entrance as a
signal that I wanted to enter. A call, "Come in,"
responded, and I crept in. A soldier, seated on the
ground, was writing home by a small tallow candle,
and I knew that any soldier was in an accessible
mood when thinking of his home. So I talked with
him about home. A sister, a devoted Christian, was,
he said, very dear to him. She had urged him to
yield himself to Christ, and he was writing to her
that very evening.

I felt that the occasion was a peculiar one, and I
must improve it. I urged him to a decision at that
very time, and I would not consent that he should
postpone it. I saw that all he needed was to come to
the act of decision, and there might never be a
better moment for this with him than now. So there
I remained with him, pleading for Christ until far

into the night. I knew that there would probably never be "a more convenient season" than this. And his strong New England mind evidently took in this fact. He was considering the matter well. Finally, he voluntarily knelt with me beneath that shelter tent, and deliberately consecrated himself to the Savior's care and service. At this I rejoiced with him, and thanked my God and his. Then, giving my hand to him, I went on to my quarters with a happier heart.

It was but a little while after this, that, in an engagement in which we had a part, he was killed; and as I said earnest words of prayer over the grave in which we buried him, and as I looked down into his dead face, I was glad that I waited that memorable night until he knelt by my side and gave himself up to his loving and waiting Savior.[15]

In civilian life as well as in wartime we may face opportunities where the duty of pressing for instant decision is a plain one. The following experience made a lifelong impression on the one who was privileged, because willing, to be God's representative.

One Sunday I passed with a near relative. There I met a gentleman whom I had never seen before, but who was connected with my relative. I sat with him at the table, and we had pleasant conversation. In the evening this gentleman was out at a church service, and the lady of the house was suffering with a headache. I urged her to retire, while I would sit up and close the house after the visitor came in. As I did this, I sat by the sitting-room fire, on the cold winter night. When the visitor was in, and the house was closed, we still sat together there.

He spoke of the service that he had attended, and he was evidently much impressed by the sermon.

"You don't often hear a sermon like that, especially from such a minister," he said. "The minister brought us right up face-to-face with the Judgment Seat, and there he left us. There were no soft words to ease us down, such as, 'But I trust this is not for you, my brethren.' "

Then, as if soliloquizing, as he sat there looking into the fire, he added:

*"I tell you that, in the great day, we who go over to the left hand will not feel very kindly toward the men who have glossed this thing over, when they had a chance to tell us the plain truth."*

The impressed man was much older than myself, old enough, perhaps, to be my father; but he had been brought to my side in a condition of mind to need help; and I was there to speak for Jesus. It was not a question of seniority, nor of long acquaintance, to be considered by one who represented the Eternal. Laying my hand lovingly on his knee, as he sat by my side looking thoughtfully into the fire, I said:

"My friend, what do you mean by speaking of 'we who go over to the left hand'? You belong on the right hand, and you ought to recognize this. The judge is your Savior. You ought to trust Him fully as such."

"I suppose I ought to," he responded.

"Well, do you not?"

"I can't say I do."

At this I drew my chair around so that I could look directly into his face, and I said earnestly, feeling the full force of my words:

"This is God's doing, and you must recognize it. God has brought us to this house to meet for the first time in our lives. He has planned it so that you should go out to that evening service, and hear that impressive appeal. And now, while all others in the house are asleep, you and I sit here facing the question of questions for your soul. I cannot leave you until you settle it. I speak for the Savior when I urge you to commit yourself to Him for now and forevermore."

Then, reaching out my hand, I said:

"My friend, you realize what all this means, and its importance. Now, promise me that this night, before you sleep, you will, on your knees, tell your loving, longing, waiting Savior, that you've delayed this thing altogether too long, but that you won't do so any longer. Tell Him that you trust Him because He is the Savior, and you are one whom He wants to save. Give me your hand on this, my friend, and then go to your room and do what you know to be your duty."

My companion evidently felt that it was a crisis hour with him, and he could not evade the sense of this. My hand was outstretched to him. For some time he said not a word, but I saw he was quivering with intense emotion. Meanwhile I was praying in my heart for a blessing on him in his conflict of soul. Then, with a convulsive movement that shook his strong frame, he put out his right hand and clasped mine as though it were for life. I realized that he had given himself to his Savior. Rising, I asked God's blessing on him, and bade him good night, and we parted. I went to my room for the night, and to pray for him, and he went to his room to pray for himself.

Before he came downstairs in the morning I left for my home. I never saw him again. Before the day closed he left that house for his home. By a severe railroad accident, on his way home, he was fatally injured, and soon he was with the Savior to whom he had trusted himself.[16]

Of one thing we may be sure, and we must make this unmistakably plain to those whom we would win: Jesus Christ *accepts at once.* If there is any delay, it is not of Christ's causing. This truth is not so commonly understood as we might suppose. Dr. Trumbull had presented the Gospel to another man late one evening. As they parted, Dr. Trumbull said, "Go to your room, kneel down before the Lord and tell Him that you want Him to save you."

When I met him the next morning I asked him if he had done as he promised to. As he said that he had, I inquired if he felt that the Savior had accepted him.

"I don't suppose that He has yet," was his reply.

"Why not?" I inquired.

"I don't suppose that Jesus Christ would accept me at once," he said.

"Well, then the responsibility is with Him. I don't see that you have anything more to do about it," was my reply.

"What do you mean?" he asked, with a surprised look.

"Why, if you have gone to the only Savior there is, and have offered yourself to Him, telling Him you are willing to shape your course by His directions, and He is not ready to accept you, but wants to wait a while, there seems to be nothing else for you to do."

"Do you mean," he asked, "that I ought to believe that Jesus Christ at once accepts me, and that I can fully trust Him now as my Savior?"

"That certainly is the way I understand it," I said. "I can't see any other way. It seems to be that or nothing."

"Then I'll do that," he said earnestly, and he evidently meant what he said.[17]

## Vital Importance of Follow-Up Work

We certainly have a responsibility to work for results just so long as the result does not appear in one who is still within our range of influence. The need and duty of "follow-up" work here are as vital as in every other field of effort. Our failure to follow up a preliminary endeavor, which was good as far as it went, may mean complete failure so far as that soul is concerned. Yet how few are willing to be as persistent as was a student of whom Henry Drummond told? Here is the story in Drummond's own words:

One night I got a letter from one of the students of the University of Edinburgh, page after page of agnosticism and atheism. I went over to see him, and spent a whole afternoon with him, and did not make the slightest impression. At Edinburgh University we have a Students' Evangelistic Meeting on Sunday nights, at which there are eight hundred or one thousand men present. A few nights after this, I saw that man in the meeting, and next to him sat another man whom I had seen occasionally at the meetings. I did not know his [the latter's] name, but I wanted to find out more about my skeptic, so when the meeting was over, I went up to him and said, "Do you happen to know ——?"

"Yes," he replied, "it is he that has brought me to Edinburgh."

"Are you an old friend?" I asked.

"I am an American, a graduate of an American university," he said. "After I had finished there I wanted to take a postgraduate course, and finally decided to come to Edinburgh. In the dissecting room I happened to be placed next to ——, and I took a singular liking for him. I found out that he was a man of very remarkable ability, though not a religious man, and I thought I might be able to do something for him. A year passed and he was just where I found him."

He [the skeptic] certainly was blind enough, because it was only two or three weeks before that that he wrote me that letter. "I think you said," I resumed, "that you only came here to take a year of the postgraduate course."

"Well," he said, "I packed my trunks to go home, and I thought of this friend, and I wondered whether a year of my life would be better spent to go and start in my profession in America, or to stay in Edinburgh and try to win that one man for Christ, and I stayed."

"Well," I said, "my dear fellow, it will pay you; you will get that man."

Two or three months passed, and it came to the last night of our meetings. We have men in Edinburgh from every part of the world. Every year, five or six hundred of them go out never to meet again, and in our religious work we get very close to one another, and on the last night of the year we sit down together in our common hall to the Lord's Supper. This is entirely a students' meeting. On that night we get in the members of the Theological Faculty, so that things may be done decently and in order. Hundreds of men are there, the cream of the youth of the world, sitting down at the Lord's table. Many of them are not members of the Church, but are there for the first time pledging themselves to become members of the Kingdom of God. I saw —— sitting down and handing the communion cup to his American friend. He had got his man. A week after he was back in his own country. I do not know his name. . . . He was a subject of Christ's Kingdom, doing His work in silence and in humility. A few weeks passed and —— came to see me. I said, "What do you come here for?"

He said, "I want to tell you I am going to be a medical missionary."

It was worth a year, was it not?[18]

Sometimes we may be surprised to find that one is confidently expecting to be followed up, and would lose faith in us if we disappointed him. An illustration of the importance of this kind of "follow-up" work is found in the following experience of Dr. Trumbull:

On one occasion, I met, in civilian life, a fellow officer, whom I honored and looked up to. In a strange place, we were in crowded quarters, where there was not a separate bed for each. In consequence, we two, who had slept on the field under the same blanket, shared the same hotel bed. Our army experiences made each of us more willing to consent to this arrangement than if we had not been in the army. My kneeling in prayer, before I lay down, opened the way for a close and loving talk on the precious relations which are between those who are one in Christ—a union closer than that of fellow soldiers.

My officer friend, although reverent toward Christ and his salvation, was not ready to express his personal trust in the Savior. As I tenderly urged him to commit himself to the one Savior, he confessed that he was not ready to do so, because of a reason that he deemed sufficient. As we conversed that night on the subject, he told me that if a certain state of things should ever exist, he would be ready to take the step, as he was not now. That night's conversation and my officer friend's conditional promise were stored in my mind, and he was a subject of my prayers.

As the months passed on, the state of things which he suggested as likely to change his view as to his personal duty came about. When I knew of this change in affairs, I had his promise in mind, and in the early morning I presented myself at his home.

"I told my wife that the chaplain would be up here to see me, after this," was the greeting that he gave me, as I entered his home. *What if I had failed to remember my promise at a time like this?*

That brave officer was ready to do his duty. He openly took a stand for Christ. His influence over others was great. He became known throughout the land as a Christian. If I had never been the means of winning any other to a confession of the Savior, I should feel that all my labors with individuals were more than repaid by the result of that one evening's talk with this soldier of country and of Christ.[19]

We must labor as though the whole responsibility for another's eternal choice rested upon us, while we rejoice in the knowledge that it is not we alone that work, "For it is God which worketh in you both to will and to do of his good pleasure" (Philippians 2:13).

## Questions for Study and Discussion

1. What is one of the most frequent of the encouragements in this work?
2. Why is no case ever hopeless?
3. Why are rebuffs in this work so rare?
4. Why are the mentally deficient even more likely than others to respond to the individual appeal?
5. What reason did John B. Gough give why no opportunity is too slight?
6. Why ought we really to be thinking more about the "trifling" opportunities than about the obviously greater ones?
7. Why is it that the preaching service and the prayer meeting can never take the place of individual work in winning souls?
8. When is it a duty to expect and work for an immediate result?
9. What vital truth must we make plain to those whom we would win, as to the time of Christ's acceptance?
10. When have we a duty to do "follow-up" work?

# How Our Lord
# Worked

## Questions to Ask Yourself Before You Read the Chapter

1. Which is the more important question for Christians to answer: "What would Jesus do?" or, "What would Jesus have me do?" Why?
2. How far have we reason to believe that Christ would do today, if He were a man on earth, as He did nineteen centuries ago?
3. What instances can you recall of Christ's individual work?
4. Upon which should you say the emphasis of Christ's teaching lay: death or life? Give Gospel passages in proof.
5. Under what circumstances did Christ criticize or condemn men? Cite instances.
6. What principles of individual work, as ascertained in these studies, are illustrated in Christ's work on earth? Cite an instance that illustrates each principle.

# 9
# How Our Lord Worked

IT is a truth often missed that, while we have work to do *for* Christ, we have not Christ's work to do. He did many things, some of which we ought not to do, others of which we could not do if we would. It is important to bear this in mind as we make a study of any part of our Lord's work. We are not Messiahs. We are not Saviors. We are not to seek to imitate the details of all that the Messiah and Savior did. But we are His messengers and representatives, and we must work in accordance with His principles.

Let us now test the principles that we have already found to be important in soul-winning, by ascertaining whether they seem to have the confirmation of Christ's own practice and teachings.

## The Individual in First Place

That the winning of and caring for the individual soul is the most important work in the Kingdom, given preferred place by Christ for Himself and for ourselves, we have already seen. Christ's teaching as to this is unmistakable (John 1:35–51). Seven of the eleven apostles who remained true to Him were won by the personal appeal to them as individuals; and probably the other four were—the circumstances of their

winning are not recorded. Again, the ninety and nine are to be
left in order to seek and find the one lost (Matthew 18:12, 13).
In the picture of the judgment, one's eternal life or death is
determined by the test of having ministered "unto one of the
least of these my brethren . . ." (Matthew 25:31–46). On the
evening before His crucifixion, alone in the upper room with
His trusted eleven friends, Jesus prayed to the Father in
joyous acknowledgment of the completion of the work for
which He had lived: "These [my disciples] knew that thou
didst send me; and I made known unto them thy name, and
will make it known; that the love wherewith thou lovedst me
may be in them, and I in them" (*see* John 17:25, 26). He was
not thinking now of the multitudes that He had addressed,
but of the little group of individuals that He had won; His
lifework was a success because these few had been won. And
the work for which He had come, and in which He had thus
succeeded, was the work which He committed, for its continuance, to them and to us: "and ye also shall bear witness,
because ye have been with me . . ." (John 15:27). ". . . As
my Father hath sent me, even so send I you" (John 20:21).
"Ye are my friends, if ye do whatsoever I command you"
(John 15:14). The cry of the individual rang louder and
carried more weight with our Lord than the word of the
crowd. Jesus turned from the many to ascertain the need of
one, and to meet that need (Mark 10:46–52).

## A Mission of Winning, Not of Opposing

Christ's mission was to win men to Him, not to drive them
from Him. He came not to tell chiefly about sin and death,
but about salvation and life. To dwell on the dark side drives
men from us; to dwell on the bright side draws them to us, if
they can be won at all. And we find the emphasis of the

Gospels unmistakable on this point. "In him was life; and the life was the light of men. . . . That was the true Light, which lighteth every man that cometh into the world" (John 1:4, 9). "For God sent not his Son into the world to condemn the world; but that the world through him might be saved" (John 3:17). ". . . the Father which sent me, he gave me a commandment, what I should say, and what I should speak. And I know that his commandment is life everlasting . . ." (John 12:49, 50).

Not only was the whole purpose and mission of Jesus Christ to win men, but His method of revealing His mission was to use a bait that would win at the start, if possible. He did this by the use of the two kinds of bait the value of which we have already seen: commending the good in men, rather than criticizing the evil; and giving their present interests prominent place to begin with.

## Beginning With Men's Present Interests

One of the most memorable instances of Christ's recognition of men's temporal interests as a first step in winning them to Him was that of the first miraculous draught of fishes and the call of the fisherman (Luke 5:1–11). But His resolute attention to men's temporal interests was characteristic of His entire ministry. Not only by His miracles of wholesale healing and feeding did He show this, but in numerous individual ministries as well.

With the sinful woman of Samaria who had come to draw water from the well of Jacob, He commenced with a request for a drink of water, and from that starting point of *her* interest He led her lovingly, skillfully, without any direct condemnation of her great sin, to the point where she was ready to confess her sin, to believe in His declaration of Messiahship, and to bring a whole city under His influence (John 4:5–26).

With Nicodemus, a trained and scholarly Pharisee whose chief interest was the rabbinical study of the Kingdom of God, and the Jews' place in that Kingdom, Jesus needed to use no indirect means at all, but, seizing at once upon that which interested Nicodemus most, He revealed to him his own ignorance of the Kingdom, and his need of that which Christ alone could offer. The power of conviction rather than argument comes out in verse 11: "we speak that we do know, and testify that we have seen . . ." (John 3:1–21).

The absorbing interest of the man helpless for thirty-eight years was his physical need; with that interest the Great Physician began, and led from it to a spiritual, life-bringing word (John 5:2–14).

With the multitude that had been miraculously fed, Jesus went at once to the shallow bottom of their interest—more bread—and held them absorbed until He could tell them of the true bread out of heaven, and to their cry, "Lord, evermore give us this bread," could answer with the Good News: "I am the bread of life: he that cometh to me shall never hunger; and he that believeth on me shall never thirst" (John 6:25–35).

When Jesus went to Jerusalem to attend the Feast of Tabernacles, and wanted to let His mission be known there at the center of Judaism, He worked in accordance with this same principle. "On each of its [the feast's] seven days a procession following a priest wound down the side of the temple hill to the pool of Siloam, the priest bearing a golden vessel which was filled with water at the pool. It was borne back to the temple, and poured forth, while the joyous crowd chanted the ancient words, 'With joy shall ye draw water from the wells of salvation.' " Was it strange that the audience was held with a tremendous thrill when, on "the last day, that great day of the feast, Jesus stood and cried, saying, If any man thirst, let him come unto me and drink"? (John 7:37, 38.)

Again, when He wanted to challenge the attention of the Jews, who, though under galling subjection to the earthly power of Rome, prided themselves on being intellectually and morally the freest people in the world, He proclaimed that if they would turn to Him and abide in Him, they should be made free! (John 8:31–36.)

When a heartbroken sister ran to meet Him to tell Him of her brother's death, His first word to her was to remind her lovingly of the resurrection in which she believed. From that He could tell her in whom was the hope of the resurrection for all, and it was not difficult to bring her to the confession: "thou art the Christ, the Son of God" (John 11:18–27).

Always did Jesus seem to connect Himself intimately with the interest of the person whom He hoped to help. When one of His own disciples, to whom He promised that they should follow Him where He was going, complained that they did not know the way, at once came the answer: "*I* am the way" (John 14:1–6). When that same disciple later showed that his chief interest was honest doubt over the resurrection story of the others, Jesus unhesitatingly met the doubter just where he was, and dispelled the doubt (John 20:24–29).

This principle of beginning with men's temporal interests, which our Lord made so prominent in His own work, He laid upon His disciple-representatives as He sent them forth to work for Him. They were to heal, cleanse, and bring to life, as part of their introduction to those whom they would reach for Christ (Matthew 10:8).

## Commending, Rather Than Condemning

The other bait-principle that we have studied, the use of hearty commendation, is prominent in Christ's earthly ministry. The surest way to drive men from us is to begin with

condemnation or criticism. It is not reasonable to suppose that
we can win men to ourselves or to Christ if we begin by telling
them of their sins. Christ did not work that way. He never
began His message to any individual or groups of persons by
condemnation of sin. He did not hesitate to denounce sin and
sinful persons under certain circumstances, as when His
proffered salvation had been rejected or was being actively
opposed (Matthew 11:20–24); or when religious leaders who
posed as God's representatives misrepresented God and
attacked Jesus Christ as from the devil (Matthew 12:24–37);
or when He was answering an attack of criticism by vigorous,
unanswerable countercriticism (Mark 7:1–13); or when He
chided His own disciples for certain failures after they had
been won to Him (Matthew 17:19–21; Mark 16:14). But
when Jesus set out to win a person to Himself, it seemed to be
His resolute purpose to find something in that one which He
could commend, and then to commend it in all heartiness.

For example, the men whom Jesus first invited to follow
Him undoubtedly had as glaring sins and as obvious defects as
most of us have today. Those imperfections must have been
quite as much of a trial to Jesus as our fellows' shortcomings
are to us. But He did not commence by telling them of this,
nor did He seek to help them at the outset by showing them
what was wrong with them. His first recorded word to faulty
Simon was, "Thou art Simon the son of John: thou shalt be
called Rock," as though to say, "for you deserve a stalwart
name." (*See* John 1:42.) So with another of the disciples:
There is no reason to suppose that Jesus could not have
found, and did not see, any sin in Nathanael; but instead of
condemning that which was there, Jesus' first word was in
outspoken, hearty admiration of this man, in that he was
particularly free from craftiness, or deceit (John 1:47).

The Gospels do not record our Lord's first words to each of

the twelve, but it is reasonable to believe that this method of approach was His method with them all, not excepting Judas Iscariot. Even apocryphal tradition preserves the deliberate intention of Christ to see the good in others, when it tells of a dead dog lying by the roadside, kicked aside and scorned by priest and Levite, until Jesus of Nazareth, passing by, looked at the little animal, and said gently, "His teeth are very white."

We must learn to work in that way, if we would take men alive as Christ did. We shall never lose, but always gain, in our influence for Christ, if we determinedly seek that which can be commended in one whom we would win, and speak heartily of it.

Christ's singling out of Zacchaeus, a man in whom there was evidently little that was likable, for the honor of a visit, with the confidence in the man's best side which that implied; the entire absence of any word of criticism by Christ of the much in the man's life that was open to criticism; the triumphant outburst of the man's higher nature as the result of this unexpected kind of treatment; and our Lord's hearty word of commendation closing the incident: could there be a plainer example of our Lord's endorsement of this principle of approval and commendation in soul-winning? (Luke 19:1–10.)

That scribe to whom Jesus said, after they had talked together about love as better than burnt offerings, "Thou art not far from the kingdom of God," must have had a quickened sense of the power and saving work of the young Teacher from Nazareth (Mark 12:28–34).

Over and over again Jesus strengthened faith by recognizing or commending faith. The tiny, mustard seed grain of faith that was hardly alive had, in many a soul, its first sprouting toward vigorous life because of our Lord's willingness to commend what others would have thought beneath commendation. Or again, when faith in Him was already strong, He did not hesitate to render a tribute to its nobleness which must have led it on to still deeper possibilities. Study the cases of the centurion of Capernaum (Matthew 8:5–13), the woman who touched Christ's garment in the crowd (Matthew 9:20–22), the two blind men (Matthew 9:27–29), the Canaanitish (Syro-Phoenician) woman (Matthew 15:21–28), Bartimaeus the blind beggar (Mark 10:46–52), the sinful woman at the house of Simon the Pharisee (Luke 7:36–50), the grateful leper of the border of Samaria (Luke 17:11–19).

Christ's instructions to His disciples, both the Twelve and the Seventy, were plain here also. They were to enter upon a mission primarily of winning men, not of condemning or denouncing. Their first word to any house into which they might enter was to be a salutation of peace. Only after they should be met by actual opposition were they to utter any word of disapproval (Matthew 10:11–16; Luke 10:3–11).

## Other Principles of Our Lord's Work

Jesus sought to find points of agreement with those whom He would win—therefore a fundamental principle in this work. To those to whom the law and the prophets were vital matters of religion and conduct He said, "Think not that I am come to destroy the law, or the prophets: I am not come to destroy, but to fulfil." And He enlarged upon this until there was no room for any honest doubt of His meaning (Matthew 5:17–19).

He led His followers to think most about what they *believed*, not what they were in doubt about—another cardinal principle of success in soul-winning (Matthew 16:13–20; John 9:35–38; 11:25–27).

He refused to offer "proof" to those who, He knew, had no honest desire for proof or any wish to believe in Him or to ascertain the truth. Yet He was ready to furnish proof to one who *wanted* to believe (Matthew 12:38, 39; 16:1–4; John 20:25–27).

As for the place of Scripture-quoting in soul-winning, we shall find, as we review these instances of our Lord's work, that the principle would seem to have Christ's endorsement. If the Scriptures were prominent in the interest of those whom He addressed, He recognized that interest by quoting Scripture. But if some other interest was more prominent in the immediate life of the one with whom He dealt, that other interest was given prior place at the outset.

Always His enduring purpose seemed to be to convince men and women that they were dear to Him and to the Father just as they stood: faulty, sinning, unworthy, discouraged, or hopeful, it mattered not if they would but let Him come close alongside.

## Questions for Study and Discussion

1. What is the difference between doing Christ's work, and doing work for Christ?
2. Mention your reasons for believing that our Lord gave preferred place to individual soul-winning in His own work, and that He would have us do so today.
3. Quote passages to show that Jesus came to point out the way of life, rather to condemn unto death.
4. What two kinds of bait, in the winning of men to Himself, were prominent in Jesus' work?

5. Cite instances of Jesus' use of men's present interests as bait.

6. What reason have we to believe that He specifically instructed His disciples to use the bait of men's present interests?

7. When did our Lord criticize and denounce?

8. Cite instances of His use of commendation as bait.

9. Cite instances of His use of commendation in building character or strengthening faith.

10. What shows that Christ's disciples were instructed to win at the start rather than to denounce?

11. Mention other principles of our Lord's work which should be controlling principles of our own.

12. Find your own illustrations of our Lord's use, or nonuse, of Scripture passages, and ascertain whether the principle formulated in chapter 6 would seem to have the approval of His example.

13. State the enduring purpose of Jesus' lifetime ministry.

# The Principles
# Reviewed

## Questions to Ask Yourself Before You Read the Chapter

1. What principles of successful soul-winning stand out most clearly in your mind, as the result of these studies?
2. What would you say are likely to be one's greatest encouragements in the work?
3. What are the chief incentives to doing the work?
4. What are the chief difficulties in the work?
5. Why may we properly call the work of individual soul-winning an art?
6. To what facts and factors do you attribute the superior effectiveness of individual work?

# 10
# The Principles Reviewed

I F we do not learn and practice the art of taking men alive, we shall be failures in the chief work of Christ's Kingdom on earth. In entering upon the work, we recognize three distinctive truths:

1. The work of individual soul-winning is the greatest work that God permits men to do.

2. It was Christ's own preferred method of work, as it is His preferred method for us today. For it is always the most effective way of working.

3. It is the hardest work in the world to do, and it always will be the hardest.

But it is an art of well-defined and plainly recognizable principles, which anyone may learn who is willing to pay the price in study and practice, and in which laymen and ministers are on an equal footing.

## The Three Points Proved

That individual soul-winning is the greatest work is part of the paradox-principle of the Way of Life. One is more than many. The least is the greatest. You cannot reach a thousand unless you can reach one. The greatest preaching is the preaching to an individual. The greatest preachers, pastors, evangelists, and missionaries agree as to this. General preaching is preliminary or preparatory to this end and climax of effort, individual work for individuals.

That it was Christ's preferred method in His earthly ministry is seen from a study of the Gospels and an examination of the relative results of His individual and His general work. Seven of the eleven faithful apostles were so won; so also was the last of the apostles, Paul. That it is Christ's preferred method for us today is seen from the easily proved superior effectiveness of the method in every branch of religious and secular life.

That it is the hardest work is inevitable. Because it is the most effective sort of warfare against the devil, it is the kind of effort which the devil most bitterly opposes, seeking always to persuade us away from it by the subtle, poisonous suggestion that we may harm the cause of Christ if we attempt it just now. For this reason it will never grow easy. Nor ought it to; its costliness is a secret of its effectiveness, and when it is easily done there is grave question whether it is effectively done.

## What the Work Demands

The obligation to do this work rests with equal weight upon every confessed follower of Christ. Failure here is open disloyalty to the Commission.

Individual work is simply a telling others of our experience of Christ's love, so that they may share it. Efficiency in this does not demand an expert knowledge of the Bible or of theology, nor skill and power in argument and discussion. It does call for unshaken knowledge of what Jesus Christ has done for us, and a deeply rooted purpose to share that knowledge with others. We must know Christ, and we must know the one to whom we would make Christ attractive.

The best way to begin in this work is to begin; the best time to begin is now. The only mistake we need really to fear is the mistake of holding off. There are few errors to dread *in* the work; the great error is the error of keeping out of the work.

## Unimportance of Our Feelings and Shortcomings

Our feelings must not be recognized as factors at all. Their presence or absence is to be brushed aside, ignored. Feeling like it is not the secret of success in this work; willpower, resolute intention persistently carried out, is the secret. We must and we may love those whom we do not like.

Our own personal shortcomings must not deter us. What Christ is, not what we are, is our message. We speak as saved sinners, not as superior beings. Yet the doing of this work is bound to have a powerfully uplifting influence upon the personal life and character of those who engage in it.

## The Life-Resolve

A life-resolve that every Christian worker ought to consider is the following: "Whenever I am in such intimacy with a soul as to be justified in choosing my subject of conversation, the theme of themes shall have prominence between us, so that I may learn his need, and, if possible, meet it." Notice that this basis for one's efforts shuts out indiscriminate, haphazard efforts, such as approaching utter strangers with an inquiry concerning their souls; conforms to the usual and proper courtesies and conventionalities of life; respects a man's individuality; but recognizes the theme of themes as worthy

of a place in any conversation which one has the right to
direct.

## Two Baits: Present Interests, Honest Commendation

As we are face-to-face with an opportunity, our whole
attention should be centered upon the person whom we
would win—nothing else. We must seek to know him in order
to know his interests; having learned what his interests are,
we must begin by working with them just as they are, not as
we think they ought to be. This is the secret of tact: a touch
in keeping with, rather than apart from, our man's present
interests. That which we put forward, in line with his present
interests, to catch his attention and win him to us, is bait. Bait
is a prime essential in winning men to us. The first miraculous
draught of fishes is one of the striking instances of our Lord's
use of this kind of bait in winning men to Him.

Another effective kind of bait, always available, is honest
commendation. One reason for its effectiveness is its rarity.
Criticism and denunciation, no matter how glaring the other's
shortcomings may be, have no place in soul-*winning*. Denunciation does not win; it antagonizes. Our business as soul-
winners is to draw men to us, not to drive them away.
Genuine, outspoken commendation always wins.

## Seeking Common Interests

Salvation may sometimes be made attractive to men by
showing that it is just as important in this world as in the
next—indeed, that its chief value to human beings while they
are human is its present value. This will be a new thought to
many who have had mistaken, stereotyped ideas of Christian
truth. But it is in line with their present interests, which are
the only interests we have to work with.

It is important to make the way of salvation simple. "Faith is that act by which one person, a sinner, commits himself to another person, a Savior."

It is often costly work to seek and find and become deeply interested in another man's interests; but it is always possible to do this. The question is not, "Am I naturally interested in this one and his interests?" but, "Am I willing to *get* interested?" We can always get interested if we are willing to pay the price in time and effort. And the deliberate cultivating of another's interests is sure to break down opposition and win that one if persisted in.

Differences of denominational or other religious belief are never sufficient to keep two men from finding common ground, if only one of the two is determined that they shall. There are certain fundamental agreements of belief which can always be found to build upon if one resolutely seeks points of agreement rather than of difference.

We may properly identify ourselves with any interest of another's provided the doing so does not demand a lowering of one's own standards of right and duty. We must often go "far afield"; we need never "let down."

## Conviction, Not Discussion or Argument

Only Christ can safely settle questions of duty for men. One man can never settle them for another, and ought not to attempt it. Therefore discussions as to details of one's personal life or duty are to be resolutely barred out of our conversation in individual soul-winning. Failure to hold to this principle may defeat our most earnest attempts to reach others. It is our duty simply to lead men to the Savior who will be their Guide, and insist that they let Him alone tell them their further duty.

"If one is right at the center, he is likely to get right at the circumference."

Conviction as to the truth and the joy of our message—a conviction that only our own personal experience can give—is our greatest strength in this work. It is to take the place of all argument and discussion, for it is all-powerful while they are worse than weak. Men are never argued into the Kingdom of Heaven; they are often estranged from God and man by argument. But men are constantly won over to belief in, and loyalty to, the Savior, by the magnetism of the irresistible conviction of a man whose belief is beyond and above and better than argument. Our conviction may safely be twofold: conviction, of course, that what we believe is true; and conviction that the man whom we are trying to win knows it is true, no matter what he professes. For every man is made in God's image.

## Place of the Bible

Because the great majority of persons who need to be brought to Christ are not specially interested in the Bible, Bible verses are not likely to be the best bait, at the outset, for winning souls. The Bible does not, as a rule, offer common meeting ground to begin with. A Bible text is not attractive to most of those who need our help. The fact that it ought to be has nothing to do with the case. We must work with men as they are, not as they ought to be.

But the Bible is the soul-winner's indispensable equipment, even though it is not necessarily his tool. It is a Bible message that we bring, Bible truth that we present, though we shall often find it well to put it into the familiar terms of the everyday life of the one whom we would reach. We must, ourselves, know the Bible through and through. It is the

Guide Book to the Way of Life. As a rule, the Bible is to be a goal rather than the beginning of our effort with the unsaved. We must begin with their present interests; we must not rest until we have brought them to such recognition of the Book as shall give it a unique place in their lives.

## Encouragements Ever-Present

The encouragements in the work are greater than the difficulties. We have only the devil working against us; we have God working with us. A frequent surprise is the finding that God has specially prepared the way, and that someone whom we approached with reluctance has been longing to be spoken to. Special difficulties are largely in our own timorous, devil-aided imaginations. Rebuffs by those whom we would win are almost unknown.

The mentally deficient are as much entitled to the Gospel message as those who have greater temporal privileges than they, and they are surprisingly ready and competent to grasp the message and to act upon it. Surprises are in store for those who, slow to believe this, will nevertheless put it to the test. Let us never cheat a childlike, helpless soul of the message which God entrusts to us for that one, and which may bring into that life the only sunshine it has ever known.

## No Opportunity Trifling

No opportunity is so slight or trifling that it can safely be passed by. The "trifles" in this work, rejected of men, may become cornerstones in life-buildings planned by the Master Builder. If we admit, of any opportunity, that it is too trifling to use, we are sure to lose priceless opportunities. We are especially in danger of missing the opportunities that are close at hand—the commonplace, everyday openings; and in so doing to overlook the souls nearest to us who need our help. Opportunity cannot be measured by man-made rules. "It may be a small matter for you to speak the one word for Christ that wins a needy soul—*a small matter to you*, but it is *everything to him*."

A chief incentive to the persistent doing of this work is the fact that absolutely no other form of effort takes its place. Faithfulness in pulpit or Sunday school or prayer meeting is a good accompaniment of it, but never a substitute for it.

## Our Duty for Results

Seeing results in the work may or may not be our privilege. It is our duty to work for results just as long as the result does not appear and the person sought is within our sphere of influence. At times it is an evident duty to urge an immediate decision. Always we ought to make it plain that Jesus Christ accepts at once—that if there is any delay it is not of His causing. Follow-up work is particularly important. It may be supremely important; without it, all our preliminary effort may count for nothing.

## Our Lord's Enduring Purpose

A study of our Lord's ministry on earth shows that the principles here reviewed have the approval of His practice and His teachings. The enduring purpose of Jesus as a man must be our enduring purpose in this work: to get close alongside of men, just as they are, in order to show them that they are dear to us and to our Savior who would be theirs.

## Questions for Study and Discussion

1. Mention three distinctive points that characterize individual soul-winning.
2. Briefly summarize the proof of each of those three points.
3. Upon what does efficiency in the work primarily depend?
4. What place should our feelings and our shortcomings have in this work? Why?
5. What do you see in favor of the making of the life-resolve that H. Clay Trumbull made?
6. Upon what should our attention be focused as we prepare to use an opportunity in individual soul-winning?
7. What two effective kinds of bait for taking men alive can you mention?
8. How far may we properly go in identifying ourselves with another's interests for the purpose of winning him to Christ?
9. What is the best way to help a man to settle questions of the details of his personal life and duty?
10. Why are argument and discussion to be barred out of this work?
11. What twofold conviction have we the right to in this work?
12. What place has the Bible in individual soul-winning? Give your reasons fully.
13. Why are the encouragements of the soul-winner greater than his difficulties?
14. How do you account for the fact that the mentally deficient are so ready to grasp the truth of salvation?
15. What is the danger in attempting to discriminate between opportunities in this work?
16. What should be our attitude toward results?
17. What was the enduring purpose of Jesus as a Man?

# Appendix
# Hints for Group Use

**W**HILE the plan of this book is such that it may easily be used for reading without special study, or again for home study by an individual alone, it is the hope of its publisher and author that it will find its widest usefulness in group use. No individual study of this theme can hope to compare in richness of result with the study that one does in a group of interested workers and thinkers, whose experiences and opinions, brought out in free, informal conference, are sure to stimulate all to fuller understanding, keener enthusiasm, and deeper conviction.

The class group need not necessarily be large. Do not defer the formation of a class because there are "not enough." Do not be discouraged if only a few, because of rain or some other such factor, attend a meeting which promised to be larger. The rain-tested few are worth more than a fair-weather many. It was a favorite belief— half joking, half serious—of H. Clay Trumbull, that in any public meeting there is just about so much good to go around, therefore the fewer there are present, the more each one is likely to get. A group of two or three earnest souls may gain more from their study than a class of twenty or thirty less genuinely interested students. The small group always has certain advantages over the large, in its informality and unity of spirit, the opportunity of each member to take greater part in the sessions, and the opportunity which the leader has of coming close to each member.

## Getting the Students to Work

The wise and skillful leader will invariably do less talking than his class does. He will resolutely make every session a *conference*—a time when the class members and the leader confer freely with each other over the problems and truths, the principles and the methods, that are before them for that day. An enthusiastic leader may *tell* a class a great deal of interesting information, but if he does not get it back again from them, by the giving out of questions and opinions and experiences on their part, he will have *taught* them little or nothing.

For thorough work, every member of the class will have his or her own copy of this textbook, and a notebook. The questions and suggestions that appear at the beginning and the end of every chapter furnish material which the leader can readily use, if he so desires. For example, while every member of the class should, for the best results, study the "Questions to Ask Yourself Before You Read the Chapter" at the start of each chapter (being careful to do so *before* reading a word of the chapter), the leader may profitably assign certain of these preparatory questions, in advance, to different members, for them to report upon in class at the beginning of the session in which that chapter is to be studied.

Thus, at the close of the session during which chapter 1 has been studied, the leader may assign respectively to different students certain of the questions that introduce chapter 2, asking them to study and write out their answers at home before reading chapter 2, and bring those answers into class with them at the next session. Of course, the reading of a chapter may materially modify or entirely reverse one's preconceived opinions on a given point, but that fact will only make this part of the home study, and of the class session, the more interesting.

The great thing is to get the student to *do his own thinking*. That is the purpose of those preparatory questions, and it should be the ever-present purpose of the true leader. It can be accomplished in numberless ways, some of which each leader will work out for himself. But unless it is accomplished, the results of any study of this subject will fall far short of what they might be.

Urge the students to answer the questions at the end of the chapters, whether at home or in class, largely in their own words rather than in the words of the book, seeking to catch the ideas and principles presented in the book so fully that they can express them readily in their own language. Then they will have made them their own.

It will be noted that certain of the questions or topics at the ends of chapters are not strictly confined to the contents of that chapter, but call for original work, and thus furnish additional material for assigning in advance for the students' homework, when that is desired.

## Actual Soul-Winning Between Sessions

The class that is content to let its study of this theme be purely theoretical might better not study at all. Every class should be a training school for service, and every student should be hard at work in that service between sessions. The most profitable feature of class work ought to be the study, by the class, of those actual experiences in individual soul-winning which members are having between sessions, and which they report in full to the class. Let the circumstances of such cases be carefully described, with the results so far as seen, and let the class discuss the special difficulties that characterize them, the problems involved, and the methods that have been or ought to be used in dealing with them. The class session will thus have a laboratory or clinical nature the value of which cannot be overestimated. A season of prayer for those yet unreached with whom present members have worked, and for a blessing upon the study looking toward the greater efficiency of the workers in this greatest work that Christ entrusts to men, will deepen and heighten the value of every moment of such study.

The notebooks should be used freely, in class and out, by both leader and students. Questions and points that occur to one in home study should be jotted down, for class discussion; so with problems and difficulties met with in one's personal experiences.

## Encouraging Original Work

Original work by the members of the class is to be encouraged at every opportunity. Suggest their discovering other principles of successful soul-winning, in addition to those given in this book, by their own independent study of these or other experiences. Particularly should original study be done in connection with the chapter on, "How Our Lord Worked." That chapter is not intended to be at all exhaustive. It only suggests how readily these principles of soul-winning may be tested by our Lord's work and teachings. There is a wealth of opportunity to discover unworked material in this same line in the Gospels, which any class or student that is in earnest can well take advantage of.

## How Many Sessions?

The number of sessions that a class devotes to the study of this volume need not necessarily be the number of chapters in the book, ten, though that offers a course of reasonable length. Some chapters are much shorter than others and might be combined with other chapters in single lessons by those who desire to shorten the time of the course.

But for a class that is willing to devote ample time to these studies, a session of a full hour can profitably be given to each of the chapters, provided the general plan of preparation and the conduct of the session already outlined be carried out.

## Making It Personal

It is often an impressive and memorable object-lesson, when conducting any public meeting or class on this subject, to ask those to rise who were won by a sermon or a general appeal to take the final step in open confession of Christ as Savior; then to ask those to rise who were led to that step by the face-to-face, individual word of some individual. This is likely, in any small group or large audience of Christian people, to demonstrate convincingly the place of individual soul-winning as the great factor in the extension of the Kingdom on earth.

# Source Notes

## Chapter 1: The Work We Are Facing

1. Henry Clay Trumbull, *Individual Work for Individuals: A Record of Personal Experiences and Convictions* (New York: The International Committee of Young Men's Christian Associations).
2. Ibid., pp. iv–v.
3. Ibid., p. 152.
4. Ibid., pp. 3–4, 8–9.
5. Ibid., pp. 24–26; 153–154; 27–30.
6. Ibid., pp. 9–10.
7. Ibid., pp. 168–169.
8. Ibid., p. 168.

## Chapter 2: The Worker and His Equipment

1. Henry Clay Trumbull, *Individual Work for Individuals: A Record of Personal Experiences and Convictions* (New York: The International Committee of Young Men's Christian Associations), pp. 162–163.
2. Ibid., pp. 132–136.
3. Ibid., pp. 76–77.
4. Ibid., pp. 73–76.
5. S. H. Hadley, *Down in Water Street*, pp. 23–24.

## Chapter 3: Need of a Life-Resolve

1. Henry Clay Trumbull, *Individual Work for Individuals: A Record of Personal Experiences and Convictions* (New York: The International Committee of Young Men's Christian Associations), p. 12.

2. Ibid., pp. 11–12.
3. Ibid., pp. 13–14.
4. Ibid., p. 17.
5. Ibid.
6. Ibid., pp. 21–22.
7. Ibid., p. 23.

## Chapter 4: Winning at the Start

1. Henry Clay Trumbull, *Individual Work for Individuals: A Record of Personal Experiences and Convictions* (New York: The International Committee of Young Men's Christian Associations), pp. 31–32.
2. Ibid., p. 32.
3. Ibid., pp. 32–35.
4. Ibid., pp. 81–83.
5. Ibid., p. 83.
6. Ibid., pp. 83–84.
7. Ibid., pp. 84–85.
8. Ibid., p. 85.
9. Ibid., p. 86.

## Chapter 5: Seeking Common Interests

1. Henry Clay Trumbull, *Individual Work for Individuals: A Record of Personal Experiences and Convictions* (New York: The International Committee of Young Men's Christian Associations), pp. 56–58.
2. Ibid., pp. 58–61.
3. Ibid., pp. 46–52.
4. The Reverend John T. Faris, *The Sunday School Times*.
5. J. E. Hodder Williams, *The Life of Sir George Williams*, pp. 98–101.

## Chapter 7: Conviction Better Than Discussion or Argument

1. Henry Clay Trumbull, *Individual Work for Individuals: A Record of Personal Experiences and Convictions* (New York: The International Committee of Young Men's Christian Associations), pp. 61–64.

2. Ibid., pp. 65–66.
3. Ibid., pp. 66–67.
4. Ibid., pp. 177–179, 186.
5. Ibid., pp. 179–180.
6. Ibid., pp. 181–182.
7. Ibid., pp. 182–183.
8. Ibid., p. 183.
9. Ibid., p. 184.
10. Ibid., pp. 184–185.
11. Ibid., pp. 185–186.
12. Ibid., p. 77.
13. Ibid., pp. 77–79.
14. Ibid., pp. 79–80.
15. Ibid., pp. 80–81.

## Chapter 8: Encouragements and Incentives

1. Henry Clay Trumbull, *Individual Work for Individuals: A Record of Personal Experiences and Convictions* (New York: The International Committee of Young Men's Christian Associations), pp. 53–56.
2. Ibid., pp. 147–150.
3. Ibid., p. 36.
4. J. E. Hodder Williams, *The Life of Sir George Williams*, p. 249.
5. Trumbull, *Individual Work*, pp. 93–98.
6. Ibid., pp. 99–101.
7. Ibid., pp. 101–102.
8. Ibid., pp. 163–166.
9. Ibid., pp. 175–176.
10. Ibid., p. 174.
11. Ibid., pp. 105–108.
12. Ibid., pp. 156–159.
13. Ibid., pp. 39–43.
14. Ibid., pp. 36–38.

15. Ibid., pp. 89–91.
16. Ibid., pp. 67–71.
17. Ibid., pp. 64–65.
18. George Adam Smith, *The Life of Henry Drummond*, pp. 364–366.
19. Trumbull, *Individual Work*, pp. 108–110.